FROMMER'S

WALKING TOURS

W9-ATN-805

Washington, D.C.

2nd Edition

Rena Bulkin

MACMILLAN • USA

ABOUT THE AUTHOR

Rena Bulkin began her travel-writing career when she set out for
Europe in search of adventure. She found it writing about hotels
and restaurants for the *New York Times* International Edition. She
has since authored 15 travel guides to far-flung destinations.

MACMILLAN TRAVEL

A Simon & Schuster Macmillan Company
1633 Broadway
New York, NY 10019

ISBN 0-02-860471-7
ISSN 1081-3373

Editor: Cheryl Farr
Map Editor: Douglas Stallings
Design by Amy Peppler Adams—designLab, Seattle
Maps by Ortelius Design

Manufactured in the United States of America

CONTENTS

Take Blue to Smithsonian (Castle)
Exit on Independence (Haupt Garden)
Go left down Jefferson. Round bldg on right
Sunken Sculpture Garden on left.
National Air & Space Museum (movie)
[Cross mall to Nat'l Gallery (W) (EAT)

Follow Independence to Bartholdi
Park (R) & Botanic Garden (L)
 Tour Capitol. See Statuary
 Old Supreme Court chamber &
 the "Crypt", Senate & House
On 1st St is Library of Congress &
Supreme Court.
Go N. on Delaware Ave to Union Station
[eat at America or another

Take Red (Shady Grove) back to
Metro Center. (Get on Blue (Addison)
to Smithsonian. Take Jefferson to
15th St (by Bureau of Engraving) to
Jefferson Memorial. Return to
Smithsonian.) Get on Blue (Franconia)

LIST OF MAPS

The Walking Tours

An Invitation to the Reader

In researching this book, I discovered many wonderful places. I'm sure you'll find others. Please tell us about them, so we can share the information with your fellow travelers in upcoming editions. If you were disappointed with a recommendation, we'd love to know that, too. Please write to:

Rena Bulkin
Frommer's Walking Tours: Washington, D.C.
Macmillan Travel
1633 Broadway
New York, NY 10019

An Additional Note

Please be advised that travel information is subject to change at any time. The author, editor, and publisher cannot be held responsible for the experiences of readers while traveling. Your safety is important to us, however, so we encourage you to stay alert and be aware of your surroundings. Keep a close eye on cameras, purses, and wallets, all favorite targets of thieves and pickpockets.

INTRODUCING WASHINGTON, D.C.

Washington, D.C., is a capital worthy of a great nation—a federal showplace of magnificent museums and gleaming marble monuments, of imposing neo-classic government buildings and verdant parklands. Spacious tree-lined thoroughfares radiate from circular plazas that are centered on splashing fountains, monuments, and statuary. Designed by a Frenchman (Pierre Charles L'Enfant), Washington more closely resembles Paris than any other American city. And like Paris, it is a delight for walkers.

ATHENS ON THE POTOMAC

Part of Washington's appeal is its architecture, which ranges from the Federal-style homes of Georgetown to the neoclassic museums and federal buildings that line the Mall. The three major houses of government are all splendid edifices. The White House was designed by Dublin architect James Hoban after the country estate of an Irish duke. Hoban received the commission as winner of a design contest that challenged participants to create a "presidential palace" with "a grandeur of conception, a Republican simplicity, and . . . true elegance of proportion." The gleaming white-domed Capitol—which is, along with the

1

Washington Monument and Lincoln Memorial, among the city's most cogent symbols—sits majestically atop a hill that L'Enfant called "a pedestal waiting for a monument." And the Supreme Court—a Corinthian marble palace designed by noted architect Cass Gilbert—is the quintessence of classical dignity.

Equally impressive are the grounds surrounding this triumvirate. They were designed by America's greatest landscapist, Frederick Law Olmsted, to include a virtual arboretum planted with thousands of trees from four continents—magnolias, giant sequoias, Belgian elms, dogwoods, crabapples, gingkos, and Japanese cherry trees among them.

Olmsted also landscaped the grounds of the Italian Renaissance–style Thomas Jefferson Building (1897) of the Library of Congress. It's one of the world's most beautiful buildings, and its architectural opulence was intended to impress Europe and demonstrate that America had arrived culturally as a nation. It took dozens of painters and sculptors—among the latter Daniel Chester French, who created the memorial statue of Lincoln—eight years to complete the lavish marble interior.

Union Station, for many the gateway to this great city, exemplifies the apogee of beaux-arts neoclassicism, complete with Ionic colonnade, allegorical sculpture, and soaring dramatic archways. Noted architect Daniel H. Burnham modeled his "temple of transport" after the Baths of Diocletian and the Arch of Constantine in Rome. Its adjacent contemporary (both were built around the turn of the century), the Old Post Office Building—its exterior embellished by fancy stonework, massive arches, and turrets—was inspired by the Romanesque cathedrals of 12th-century France.

John Russell Pope designed three of the city's most noted neoclassic beauties—the Jefferson Memorial, the National Gallery of Art, and the National Archives. In the same genre, the Lincoln Memorial, a Doric-columned Greek Temple, looks out over the stark white marble obelisk of the Washington Monument.

The above list is just a brief sampling of the notable buildings and monuments you'll see on these tours. Many of them have more than aesthetic significance to Americans; they represent, in stone and marble, the spirit of democracy and the highest aspirations of a nation. Similarly, the newer Vietnam Memorial is a powerful evocation of the tragedy of all wars; few people can walk its length without being moved to tears.

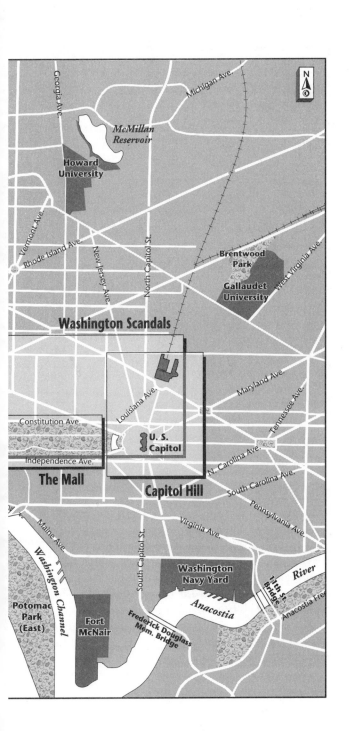

A tireless lobbyist for municipal improvements, he fought successfully for the creation of an illustrious committee—composed of landscapist Frederick Law Olmsted, sculptor Augustus Saint-Gaudens, and architects Daniel Burnham and Charles McKim—to create "the city beautiful." At his own expense, McMillan sent this blue-ribbon panel to Europe for seven weeks to study the landscaping and architecture of that continent's great capitals. It was a committee worthy of L'Enfant's vision, backed by the necessary political clout to get the job done. Burnham summed up the committee's vitality when he counseled, "Make no little plans. They have no magic to stir men's blood, and probably themselves will not be realized. Make big plans, aim high in hope and work, remembering that a noble and logical diagram once recorded will never die, but long after we are gone will be a living thing, asserting itself with ever growing insistency." The McMillan Commission returned to make big plans— and bring them to fruition. They developed a system of parks for the city, selected sites for government buildings, beautified the Mall, and created the Lincoln and Jefferson Memorials, the Arlington Memorial Bridge, Union Station, and a reflecting pool (between the Washington Monument and the Lincoln Memorial) modeled after the one at Versailles.

A later Commission of Fine Arts, again with Olmsted as a member, was appointed in 1910 under President Taft to further create monuments, fountains, and neoclassical buildings. It was also under Taft that the famous cherry trees—a gift from Japan—were planted around the Tidal Basin.

AMERICA'S MUSEUM MECCA

Today there are 11 major Smithsonian museums in Washington, exhibiting everything from scientific specimens and spacecraft to great works of art encompassing all nations and historical periods. Smithson's original bequest has been multiplied many times by philanthropists like Joseph Hirshhorn, Arthur M. Sackler, and Charles Lang Freer, who donated their collections—and funds to house them—to the nation's capital.

At the National Air and Space Museum, you can explore the history of aviation from the Wright brothers' 1903 flyer and the *Spirit of St. Louis* to lunar exploration vehicles. The National Museum of American History examines "everyday life in our American past," with displays ranging from a Revolutionary War general's tent to Archie Bunker's chair. Fossils, evolution, gems and minerals, dinosaurs, insects, birds and animals, and anthropology are among the focuses of the National Museum of Natural History. Two art museums—the National Museum of American Art and the National Portrait Gallery—share the palatial quarters of the Old Patent Office Building (designed by Robert Mills, whose credits also include the Washington Monument). The Arthur M. Sackler Gallery and the Freer Gallery of Art concentrate on Asian art from thousands of years B.C. through the present (the Freer also owns over a thousand works by American artist James McNeill Whistler). And the adjoining National Museum of African Art highlights the vast sub-Saharan region of that continent. Modern art is the province of the Hirshhorn Museum and its delightful Sculpture Garden. The Renwick Gallery (actually part of the Museum of American Art) is a national showcase for American crafts. The palatial National Postal Museum displays the Smithsonian's philatelic and postal history collection of more than 16 million objects (surprise! it's fascinating). And the 1876 United States International Exposition in Philadelphia is re-created in all its Victorian splendor in the red brick and sandstone Arts and Industries Building. Don't expect to see it all in one trip. Touring the Smithsonian museums can take a lifetime. And in addition to the Smithsonian, there are nearly a dozen other noteworthy museums in Washington, among them the National Gallery of Art.

WASHINGTON ALFRESCO

No less a thrill than the city's architecture is its exquisite landscaping. Thousands of cherry trees—12 different varieties—adorn Potomac Park's riverside with clouds of delicate pink-and-white blossoms every spring.

Rock Creek Park is one of the largest and most beautiful urban parks in America. Created in 1890, it was purchased by Congress for its "pleasant valleys and ravines, primeval forests and open fields, its running waters, its rocks clothed with rich ferns and mosses, its repose and tranquillity, its light and shade, its ever-varying shrubbery, its beautiful and extensive views." It comprises wooded hiking trails, unspoiled wilderness (you can often spot deer in more remote sections), stands of pine and cypress, old forts to explore, shady bridal trails, and sports facilities. There's a marvelous 11-mile paved bike route from the

Lincoln Memorial through the park into Maryland. And the National Zoo, which is part of the Smithsonian, is adjacent to the park.

Another great outdoor joy is the Chesapeake & Ohio Canal National Historic Park—a $184^{1}/_{2}$-mile towpath paralleling the Potomac—just a block off Georgetown's main street.

Washington also boasts a national botanic garden and a stunning arboretum (viewing the bonsai collection here is a spiritual experience), not to mention Dumbarton Oaks' 10 acres of enchanting formal gardens in Georgetown. And natural beauty abounds throughout the capital city—from the spring plantings of Lafayette Square, to tranquil tree-shaded streets, to apartment buildings fronted by charming flower gardens.

AND A LITTLE HISTORY

The tours outlined in this book also take you back in time. In Georgetown—a tobacco port predating Washington, D.C., with many 18th- and 19th-century mansions still intact—you'll amble through a scenic Victorian cemetery; visit Dumbarton Oaks, site of the 1944 international conference that led to the formation of the United Nations; and tour a home that was visited by Robert E. Lee, Henry Clay, Daniel Webster, and John Calhoun.

Alexandria, Virginia—hometown of George Washington and Robert E. Lee—has a large restored district (the Old Town) with over 2,000 historic buildings lining its cobblestone streets. Here you'll visit a tavern where George and Martha Washington danced and patriots plotted the American Revolution.

For its architecture, its natural beauty, its culture, and historic significance, we're sure you'll enjoy your walks in Washington, as well as those in noteworthy towns nearby. Of course, Washington isn't all gorgeous buildings and gardens. As columnist Russell Baker once noted, many Americans view the Federal City as "an unworthy place where men of mean talents but cunning proclivities conspire to inconvenience decent people beyond its frontiers." With that darker view in mind, I've also included a tour of famous Washington scandal sites. I guarantee you're going to love this town.

THE MALL

Start: Smithsonian Information Center (the "Castle").

Metro: Smithsonian (cross Jefferson Drive and look for the red sandstone "Castle" to your left).

Finish: National Museum of American History.

Time: Approximately 2 to 3 hours, depending on browsing stops.

Best Times: Any daytime. All attractions listed here are open seven days a week, most of them from 10am to 5:30pm.

In Pierre Charles L'Enfant's original plan for Washington, D.C., the Mall was conceived as a wide ceremonial avenue lined with embassies and other distinguished buildings. Of course, L'Enfant could not have envisioned that in 1829 James Smithson, an English scientist, would bequeath $500,000 "to found at Washington an establishment for the increase and diffusion of knowledge. . . ." Hence, Smithsonian museums have become the "distinguished buildings" lining the Mall, while embassies have situated themselves along Massachusetts Avenue.

The immense scope of the Smithsonian can be intimidating to tourists. I've heard out-of-towners in hotel lobbies planning to "do the Smithsonian today." Actually, you couldn't see all of the Smithsonian in several lifetimes, since only about one

ings are on display at any given time and ex-
larly. Also, to tour more than one or two of
ries in a day would be exhausting. Though
to resist a bit of browsing, this tour is not
designed for serious museum-going. It is meant instead as an
orientation to the layout of the Mall with future exploration in
mind.

• • • • • • • • • • • • • • • •

1. **Smithsonian "Castle,"** 1000 Jefferson Drive SW. Before you go inside, stand across the street from the main
entrance to appreciate the beauty of the building. James
Renwick's Victorian red sandstone "castle" (1847–55), with
its octet of crenellated Norman towers, was the Institution's
first edifice. Originally, it served as a home for the first secretary of the Smithsonian and contained all of the
Institution's operations and collections. Today its Great Hall
houses the Smithsonian Information Center, where informational exhibits about the complex include a 20-minute
video that runs throughout the day, large schematic models
of the Mall, dozens of interactive video machines with
extensive data menus, and a large light-up map of Washington sights. The Smithson crypt is to your right as you
enter. The castle is fronted by a lovely flower garden. Its
Jefferson Avenue entrance is via the ornate Oriental-style
Children's Room, which was designed to interest young
people in the natural sciences. In this utterly delightful room,
a gilt-trimmed ceiling is decorated to represent a grape
arbor (brightly plumed birds and blue sky peek through
trellising). Furnishings are peacock-themed, and large
Chinese paintings adorn the walls.

A multilingual staff is on hand to answer all your
questions, and daily Smithsonian events are displayed on
monitors. Do stop in to acquaint yourself with this excellent resource; it opens at 9am daily.

Walk through the "Castle" and exit via its Independence
Avenue portal (actually the main entrance) into the beautiful Enid A. Haupt Garden, a peaceful setting of magnolias,
hollies, hybrid tea roses, wisteria-covered arbors, and
magnolia-lined parterres planted with swags and ribbon beds

A "Liberal and Enlightened Donor"

Wealthy English scientist James Smithson (1706–1829), the illegitimate son of the Duke of Northumberland, never explained why he willed his vast fortune to the United States—a country he had never visited. Speculation is that he felt a new nation, lacking established cultural institutions, stood in greatest need of his bequest. Smithson died in Genoa, Italy, in 1829. Congress accepted his gift in 1836; two years later a shipment of 105 bags of gold sovereigns (about half a million dollars' worth—a considerable sum in the 19th century) arrived at the United States Mint in Philadelphia. For the next eight years Congress debated the best possible use for these funds. Finally, in 1846, James Polk signed an act into law establishing the Smithsonian Institution and providing "for the faithful execution of said trust, according to the will of the liberal and enlightened donor." It authorized a board to receive "all objects of art and of foreign and curious research, and all objects of natural history, plants, and geological and mineralogical specimens . . . for research and museum purposes."

In addition to the original Smithson bequest—which has been augmented by many subsequent endowments—the Smithsonian is also supported by annual congressional appropriations. Today it comprises a complex of 14 museums, nine of them on the Mall, plus the National Zoological Park. Its holdings—in every area of human interest—total more than 140 million objects and specimens, running the gamut from a 3.5-billion-year-old fossil to part of a 1902 Horn & Hardart Automat. Additionally, the Smithsonian has sponsored thousands of scientific expeditions that have pushed into remote frontiers in deserts, mountains, polar regions, and jungles.

An interesting note: Alexander Graham Bell was the regent charged with bringing Smithson's remains to the United States from Italy in 1904. The remains were reinterred in a chapel-like room of the Smithsonian "Castle."

adapted from the 1876 Philadelphia Centennial Exposition's horticultural hall. The setting is enhanced by cast-iron Victorian furnishings, plant-filled urns, and lush baskets hung from old-fashioned lampposts. An Islamic summer garden, with a waterfall or "chadar" evocative of the gardens of Shalimar, harmonizes with the adjacent National Museum of African Art. And a moon gate garden—inspired by the Temple of Heaven in Beijing, with bridges suspended over a pool, benches backed by English boxwoods, and weeping Japanese cherry trees—complements (on your right) the:

2. **Arthur M. Sackler Gallery,** 1050 Independence Avenue SW. Opened in 1987 and named for psychiatrist/medical researcher Arthur M. Sackler, who contributed the nucleus of its permanent collection, this subterranean museum (96% of the building's exhibition space is underground) focuses on the arts of Asia. For the most part, The Sackler presents traveling exhibits from major cultural institutions in Europe, Asia, and the United States. In past years, such exhibits have focused on themes ranging from Chinese porcelain to the opulent courts of Indonesia. These shows are supplemented by changing exhibits from the permanent collection, which includes Chinese paintings, bronzes, jade figures, and lacquerware spanning the millennia from 3000 B.C. to the present; significant collections of Japanese and Islamic art; and 11th- to 19th-century Persian and Indian paintings and manuscripts.

Architecturally notable, the Sackler has a pyramidal silhouette designed to harmonize with the Victorian Arts and Industries Building. Its subterranean spaces are enhanced by vast skylights, lush plantings, and indoor fountains. The Sackler connects via an underground exhibit space with the:

3. **Freer Gallery of Art,** Jefferson Drive and 12th Street SW. Charles Lang Freer, a Detroit railroad-car manufacturer and collector of Asian and American art, donated his collection of 9,000 works to the Smithsonian—along with funding to construct a building to house it—in 1906. The first of the Smithsonian art museums, the Freer Gallery opened in 1923. In the Asian collection—which, partly thanks to additional Freer funding, has been greatly

The Mall

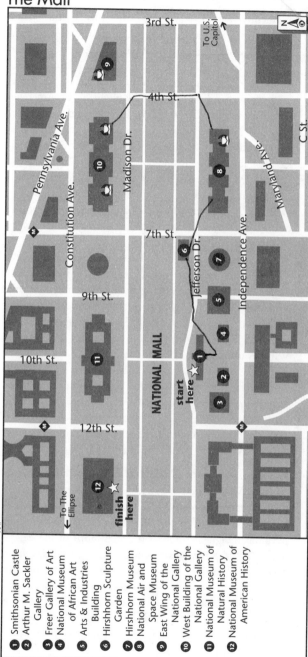

1. Smithsonian Castle
2. Arthur M. Sackler Gallery
3. Freer Gallery of Art
4. National Museum of African Art
5. Arts & Industries Building
6. Hirshhorn Sculpture Garden
7. Hirshhorn Museum
8. National Air and Space Museum
9. East Wing of the National Gallery
10. West Building of the National Gallery
11. National Museum of Natural History
12. National Museum of American History

augmented over the years—are early Christian illuminated manuscripts; Chinese and Japanese lacquer, metalwork, sculpture, and ceramics; Korean ceramics; Chinese jades and bronzes; Near Eastern manuscripts and miniatures; Japanese screens and woodblock prints; and Indian sculpture, manuscripts, and paintings. A highlight of the American collection is over 1,200 works by Freer's friend and mentor James McNeill Whistler. Among the Whistler holdings is the Peacock Room, a reassembled interior Whistler created for the home of his patron Frederick Leyland in the 1870s. Actually, Whistler was merely commissioned to create a painting for the room *(The Princess from the Land of Porcelain)*. However, when his painting was installed, he deemed the room an unsatisfactory setting for his *oeuvre.* Without Leyland's permission (he was traveling at the time), Whistler flamboyantly embellished the room's expensive gilded-leather walls with golden peacocks. This creative act resulted in a permanent estrangement between Leyland and Whistler. Other highlights of the American collection include works by Thomas Wilmer Dewing, Childe Hassam, and John Singer Sargent. Exquisite frames designed by Whistler or noted architect Stanford White enhance many of the American works. The marble museum building, designed by architect Charles A. Platt, resembles an Italian Renaissance palazzo, with galleries centered on a skylit garden courtyard.

Walk back through the Sackler and Enid A. Haupt Garden to the side entrance of the:

4. **National Museum of African Art,** 950 Independence Avenue SW. Founded in 1964, the NMAA became part of the Smithsonian in 1979 and, like the Sackler, opened on the Mall in 1987. It, too, is subterranean, with domed pavilions designed to reflect the arch motif of the neighboring Freer. Shown in rotating exhibits, its permanent collection of over 7,000 objects—most of them from the 19th and 20th centuries—highlights the traditional arts of the vast sub-Saharan region. Additional holdings include the Eliot Elisofon Photographic Archives, 300,000 photographic prints and transparencies and 120,000 feet of film relating to African arts and culture.

Exit the NMAA via the same door you entered, turn right on the brick path, and take the next right to the side entrance of the:

5. **Arts and Industries Building,** Jefferson Drive and Ninth Street SW. The second-oldest of the Smithsonian buildings, this Victorian Romanesque red-brick and sandstone structure opened its doors in 1881, just in time for President James Garfield's inaugural ball. The building originally housed exhibits from the 1876 United States International Exposition in Philadelphia, a centennial fair that celebrated America's coming of age. Much of the Exposition display was re-created for the Bicentennial in 1976 and has remained in place ever since. The building's hub is a vast skylit rotunda over a fountain, with four lofty-ceilinged halls radiating from it. Exhibits run the gamut from Victorian furnishings to state and international displays, along with weaponry, 19th-century machinery, corn mills, and vehicles such as a steam locomotive. *Note:* There has recently been some talk about replacing this Bicentennial exhibition, so perhaps by the time you visit something new will have been installed.

Exit on Jefferson Drive and make a right. When you come to the Hirshhorn, a circular building, cross the street to the:

6. **Hirshhorn Museum's magnificent sunken Sculpture Garden,** which contains, among other works, Rodin's *The Burghers of Calais.* Other highlights are Thomas Eakins' bronze bas reliefs *The Continental Army Crossing the Delaware* and *The Battle of Trenton;* Rodin's *Monument to Balzac;* four Matisse bronze bas reliefs called *The Backs;* Miró's *Lunar Bird;* and Picasso's *Pregnant Woman.* Works by Bourdelle, Maillol, Arp, Baskin, Lipchitz, Epstein, Lachaise, Manzu, and Giacometti are also displayed here, and a Calder adjoins a reflecting pool. Do take some time to explore this enchanting outdoor facility.

Return to Jefferson Drive, cross the street (walking back in the direction of the Arts and Industries Building), and make your first left (a brick path) through the Ripley Garden—yet another gorgeous garden on the Mall. It takes you to the Independence Avenue entrance of the:

7. **Hirshhorn Museum.** This doughnut-shaped concrete-and-granite building—sheltering a verdant courtyard plaza, which, like the above-described garden, is used to display sculpture—is an important repository of 20th-century art. In 1966, Latvian-born immigrant Joseph H. Hirshhorn (who made his fortune in uranium mining) donated his vast modern art collection to the United States "as a small repayment for what this nation has done for me and others like me who arrived here as immigrants." Hirshhorn's original gift—more than 4,000 contemporary paintings and drawings and 2,000 pieces of sculpture, the latter including the country's largest number of works by Henry Moore—was augmented at his death by a bequest of an additional 5,500 works. Since then, numerous other donors have further expanded his legacy. Just about every prominent 20th-century artist is represented here. A rotating show of about 600 works is on view at all times.

Exit on Independence Avenue and turn left. Next stop is the three-block-long:

8. **National Air and Space Museum,** between Seventh and Fourth Streets SW, where exhibits ranging from the *Spirit of St. Louis* to the Skylab orbital workshop (you can walk through and see how astronauts lived in orbit) chronicle man's mastery of flight. Almost all of the over 300 historic or technologically significant aircraft—and 150 spacecraft—on display are originals. Other displays, many of them interactive, include a touchable moon rock collected by *Apollo 17* astronauts from the lunar surface, aerospace computers, exhibits on the history of aviation, and weather and space satellites. A planetarium and IMAX movie theater (where thrilling 70-millimeter films are projected on a special five-story screen) are on the premises; if you're getting foot-weary, consider resting up at a show.

☕ **Take a Break** **The Wright Place,** in the National Air and Space Museum, is an attractive full-service restaurant enclosed by a chrome railing and greenery. Floor-to-ceiling windows provide great Mall views. Fare is American/continental; entrées range from a three-cheese pizza to hearty Brunswick stew served with salad and fresh-baked corn muffins. Wine and microbrewery beers are available. Prices are moderate. Open daily from 11:30am to 3pm.

On the floor below The Wright Place is **Flight Line,** a cheerful glass-enclosed cafeteria carpeted in forest green with seating at marble-topped pine tables. Sunshine streams in through windowed walls. Inexpensive sandwiches, salads, and entrées (pastas, pizzas, chili, burgers, lasagne, meatloaf) are offered daily from 10am to 5pm.

Turn left on Fourth Street. Cross the Mall (note the Capitol and Washington Monument at opposite ends of the Mall's central pathway). on your right you'll see the:

9. **East Wing of the National Gallery.** Though related to it in some arcane way, the National Gallery is not a Smithsonian Museum. The ultramodern honeycombed triangular East Building, with its great glass walls and tetrahedron skylights, was designed by I. M. Pei. Opened in 1978, it focuses on 20th-century art and features important changing exhibits.

Across Fourth Street on Madison Drive, the neo-classical: ON LEFT

10. **West Building,** with its domed rotunda and colonnaded garden courts, was designed by John Russell Pope (1941), architect of the Jefferson Memorial. Its collections encompass all the great historic periods of European and American art, with exhibition rooms decorated to reflect the period and country of the works displayed. About 1,000 paintings are always on exhibit on the main floor, where galleries off the rotunda feature 17th- to 19th-century American and British artists; Italian paintings spanning the Renaissance through the 18th century (including the only Leonardo da Vinci outside Europe, *Ginevra de'Benci*); the Germans (Grünewald, Dürer, Holbein, Cranach); the Spanish (El Greco, Goya, Velázquez); the Flemish (Van Eyck, Rubens, Bosch); and the Dutch—most notably a fine collection of Rembrandts.

Take a Break There are two delightful full-service restaurants in the National Gallery complex, both of which provide restful settings and American/continental fare at reasonable prices. They are the fern- and flower-bordered

<u>Garden Café</u> in the West Building (my favorite), with tables under a skylight arranged around a marble fountain, and the **Terrace Café** in the East Building, offering views of the Mall. Menus change frequently; both serve items such as poached salmon on a bed of spinach pasta. In addition, there's the **Concourse Buffet** (in the concourse that connects the East and West wings), a cheerful cafeteria with seating amid planters and potted palms. The Terrace and Garden Cafés are open Monday through Saturday from 11:30am to 3pm, Sunday from noon to 4 and 6:30pm, respectively. Concourse Buffet hours are Monday through Saturday from 10am to 3pm, Sunday from 11am to 4pm.

Continue walking west on Madison Drive (toward the Washington Monument) past the circular ice skating rink to the:

11. **National Museum of Natural History.** Stuffed birds and animals, a 70-million-year-old dinosaur egg, thousands of fossils chronicling the evolution of marine life, Ice Age mammals, a 3,000-gallon tank containing a living coral reef, and the Hope Diamond are just a few of the 120 million artifacts and specimens on display here. Anthropological exhibits explore African, Asian, Pacific, and other diverse cultures. You can observe the workings of a leaf-cutter ant colony in the museum's Insect Zoo, and learn about the world's largest invertebrates in an exhibit called "In Search of the Giant Squid." If you have the energy, since we're close to the end of our walk, pick up a self-guided audio tour at the Rotunda information desk and view the major exhibits.

Continue west along Madison Drive to the:

12. **National Museum of American History,** which deals with "everyday life in the American past." Exhibits run a wide gamut. Some examples: Alexander Graham Bell's experimental telephone; the original star-spangled banner that inspired Francis Scott Key to write the American national anthem in 1814; a collection of First Ladies' gowns; a reassembled 19th-century West Virginia post office and country store; a 1926 steam locomotive; a fallout shelter from Indiana; ship models; weaponry; textiles; timepieces from sundials to atomic clocks—even Archie Bunker's

favorite chair. Do stop in to see the Foucault Pendulum (directly across from the entrance), a thrilling exhibit illustrating the rotation of the earth. A heavy pendulum, suspended from the roof, swings from side to side in an unvarying arc, knocking over, one by one, a circle of pegs on the floor beneath it. The pendulum doesn't change its arc; rather, the floor moves as the earth rotates. The original Foucault Pendulum was exhibited in Paris in 1851 with the accompanying teaser, "You are invited to witness the earth revolve."

MONUMENTS & MEMORIALS

Start: The John F. Kennedy Center for the Performing Arts.

Metro: Foggy Bottom. When you exit the Metro, make an immediate right into I Street (a walkway), then turn left onto New Hampshire Avenue and follow it to the end. Cross Virginia Avenue and take the path behind the statue of Benito Juarez to the Hall of States building.

Finish: Washington Monument.

Time: Approximately 3 hours, not including the Kennedy Center tour.

Best Times: Monday to Friday, avoiding weekend crowds.

Only three of America's past presidents have been singled out for recognition with great monuments in the capital city—George Washington, Thomas Jefferson, and Abraham Lincoln. Two other notable monuments here are the Kennedy Center, honoring President John F. Kennedy, and the Vietnam Veterans Memorial, commemorating those who gave their lives in the Vietnam War, the longest war in America's history. All of these major sightseeing attractions are conveniently grouped to be seen on a walking tour, though it is a fairly long walk.

An alternative to walking is to take the Tourmobile, an open-air sightseeing bus that stops at all of the below-listed places. For a single fare, you can board at any stop, staying as long as you like and catching the next bus that comes along when you're ready to move on. The buses travel in a loop, serving each stop every 20 to 30 minutes. Call 202/554-5100 for details. (You could also walk most of the tour and hop a taxi if you get tired.)

• • • • • • • • • • • • • • • • •

Starting Out   The most delightful way to begin this tour is with breakfast at **Palladin** in the Watergate Hotel, 2650 Virginia Avenue NW (tel. 202/298-4455). Under the auspices of one of America's premier chefs, Jean-Louis Palladin, this eponymous eatery is just as lovely as it can be. It doesn't come cheap, but the fare is excellent and the ambience idyllic. Choices range from continental fare (brioches, croissants, and the like) to pancakes, eggs Benedict, even a full Japanese breakfast. Palladin is open for breakfast daily from 7 to 10:30am. It's also a good choice for lunch (Monday through Saturday from 11:30am to 2:30pm), featuring salads, sandwiches (perhaps farm-raised roast chicken with fennel and confit of tomatoes on a rustic baguette), and entrées such as fresh Virginia softshell crab with crispy pancetta. Menus change frequently. Sundays (same hours) there's a prix-fixe champagne buffet brunch.

Another elegant option is the **Roof Terrace Restaurant** in the Kennedy Center (tel. 202/416-8555), with Louis XV–style furnishings under a lofty crystal-chandeliered ceiling. Menus change seasonally; you might lunch on crabcakes with green herb aïoli, a Caesar salad with mesquite-grilled chicken, or a Monterey Jack cheeseburger with shoestring fries. A full lunch here runs about $20 per person. It's served on matinee performance days only (call ahead). Every Sunday, the Roof Terrace features a lavish prix-fixe buffet brunch from 11:30am to 3pm; an à la carte menu is also available.

The Encore Café (tel. 202/416-8560), is a less glamorous—and less expensive—option. It's an attractive cafeteria, with comfortable seating amid ficus trees and windows providing gorgeous city views. Choices include entrées such as crabcakes, pizza, lasagne, and chili, along with sandwiches, salads, and fresh-baked desserts. Wine and beer are available. Open daily from 11am to 8pm.

Begin at the:

1. **John F. Kennedy Center for the Performing Arts.**
A performing arts center for the nation's capital was conceived, surprisingly, under the rather anti-intellectual Eisenhower administration in 1958. Seventeen acres overlooking the Potomac were alloted for it. During his presidency, John F. Kennedy was very involved with the project. But it was President Lyndon Johnson who finally authorized the necessary funding in a bill that specified the name of the complex and defined it as a living memorial to JFK.

The plush $73-million facility, an affiliate of the Smithsonian, opened September 8, 1971 with a performance of Leonard Bernstein's *Mass*. Designed by Edward Durrell Stone (also the architect of New York's Museum of Modern Art), it contains an opera house, a concert hall, two dramatic theaters, and a film theater. JFK quotations—such as "The New Frontier for which I campaign in public life can also be a New Frontier for American Art"—are carved into the building's facade. Within, you'll see the gifts of many nations, such as Matisse tapestries from France, silk furnishings from Thailand, an Egyptian alabaster vase dating from 2600 B.C., and crystal chandeliers from Sweden. Italy donated the marble of which the building is constructed.

The best way to see it all, including areas you can't visit on your own, is to take one of the free 45-minute tours offered daily, on a continual basis between 10am and 1pm. After 1pm you can pick up a self-guided tour brochure at the information desk. Call 202/416-8340 for details. Do be sure to walk the upper-level promenade that girds the building for magnificent city and river views.

Monuments & Memorials

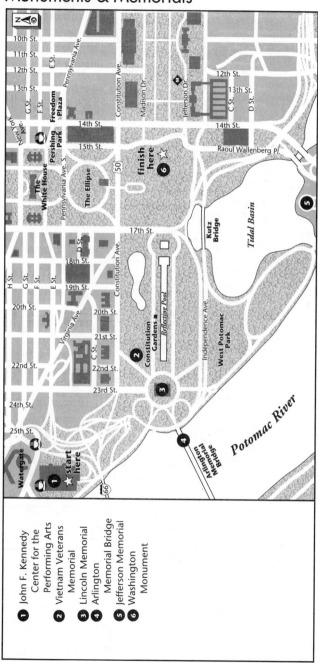

1 John F. Kennedy Center for the Performing Arts
2 Vietnam Veterans Memorial
3 Lincoln Memorial
4 Arlington Memorial Bridge
5 Jefferson Memorial
6 Washington Monument

Walk back the way you came in, making a right on Virginia Avenue (follow the pointing statue of Benito Juarez), then another right on 23rd Street. Note the beautiful hilltop homes on your right; they belong to Navy brass. On your left, just north of C Street, you'll pass the State Department. (The entrance is around the corner to your left on C Street; you might want to peek into the lobby, where flags of all countries that maintain diplomatic relations with the U.S. are displayed.) Cross Constitution Avenue, make a left, walk past Henry Bacon Drive, and follow the signs to the:

2. **Vietnam Veterans Memorial.** This moving tribute to the men and women who served in the armed forces during the Vietnam War consists of two long black granite walls inscribed with the names of close to 60,000 Americans who died or remain missing as a result of that conflict. Their average age was 19.

The memorial was conceived by Vietnam veteran Jan Scruggs and built by the Vietnam Veterans Memorial Fund (VVMF), a non-profit organization that raised $7 million for the project. The VVMF was granted a site of two acres in Constitution Gardens for a monument that would harmonize with neighboring surroundings and make no political statement about the war.

The two sunken walls, designed by Yale architecture student Maya Ying Lin, are angled at 125 degrees to point to the Washington Monument and the Lincoln Memorial. Their mirrorlike surface reflects the surrounding trees and foliage of Constitution Gardens. Names are inscribed in chronological order, documenting the war as a series of individual sacrifices from the date of the first American casualty in 1959 to the last in 1975. Many visitors leave flowers, snapshots, poems, and other mementoes near the names of their loved ones. The wall was erected in 1982. On Veterans Day in 1984, a flagpole and a lifesize bronze sculpture of three American soldiers by Frederick E. Hart was installed at the entrance to the Plaza.

Another sculpture, the Vietnam Veterans Women's Memorial by Glenna Goodacre, was installed across from the wall on Veterans Day of 1993. It depicts two nurses tending a wounded soldier as a third scans the skies for a helicopter. At the other end of the wall you'll find a Park Service information booth, where the ranger on duty offers computer printouts of wall locations and materials for creating rubbings; he or she can locate wall honorees by name, city and state, casualty date, or military unit. The memorial is open 24 hours, with rangers on duty from 8am to midnight.

At the end of the wall, to your left, you'll see the:

3. **Lincoln Memorial.** Though planned as early as 1867, this famous landmark was not completed until 1922, a little over half a century after President Abraham Lincoln was assassinated. It occupies reclaimed land dredged from the Potomac River, a subject on which Speaker of the House "Uncle Joe" Cannon warned, "If you put it in that marsh, it will shake itself to pieces in no time with loneliness and ague."

The memorial, which has held up very nicely, thank you, was inspired by the Parthenon in Greece. Designed by Henry Bacon, it is a rectangular Doric temple with 36 marble columns (representing the 36 states that belonged to the Union when Lincoln died). Names of the 48 states in the Union, as of 1922, are inscribed toward the top of the monument, along with an Alaska and Hawaii plaque that was added later. The memorial is in perfect alignment with the Washington Monument (across the reflecting pool) and the Capitol. Inside the 100-foot structure is an awe-inspiring white marble statue of Lincoln in deep contemplation by Daniel Chester French. It is flanked by two rows of Ionic columns. Lincoln's Second Inaugural Address and Gettysburg Address are engraved on the interior walls, along with two 60-foot painted murals by Jules Guerin allegorically depicting the freeing of the slaves (Emancipation) and the unity of north and south (Reunion). Outside, the reflecting pool mirrors the Washington Monument. The memorial is open 24 hours, with rangers on duty from 8am to midnight.

Circle the monument to see the very beautiful:

4. **Arlington Memorial Bridge,** which connects Washington, D.C., with Virginia. It symbolizes the reunion of north and south after the Civil War.

Don't cross the bridge, but continue circling the Lincoln Memorial and follow the elm-shaded right-hand path of the reflecting pool. Where the pool ends, make a right and cross, past the statue of John Paul Jones, to Tidal Basin Drive, site of Washington's famous cherry trees. After you cross **Tidal Basin Drive,** you'll see Kutz Bridge. Don't cross it, but take the path that leads off its entrance to the waterside path. Turn right and follow it to the:

5. **Jefferson Memorial.** A memorial on this site—though its subject was unspecified—was mandated by the McMillan Commission, an illustrious committee formed at the turn of the century by Michigan Senator James McMillan to create "the city beautiful" in Washington, D.C. Its members included landscapist Frederick Law Olmsted (who created New York's Central Park), sculptor Augustus Saint-Gaudens, and noted architects Daniel Burnham and Charles McKim. A memorial to Jefferson on the site (land reclaimed from the Potomac River, now known as the Tidal Basin) was authorized by Congress in 1934. The cornerstone was laid by Franklin D. Roosevelt in 1939, and the memorial was dedicated on April 13, 1943, Jefferson's birthday.

There was considerable controversy over architect John Russell Pope's circular colonnaded design, because it was considered too similar to the Lincoln Memorial and would obstruct the view of the Potomac from the White House. However, Pope's conception reflected Jefferson's architectural preference for classical form, and it won the day. The central focus under the domed interior is Rudolph Evans's 19-foot bronze statue of Jefferson atop a 6-foot pedestal of black Minnesota granite. Inscriptions from Jefferson's writings are engraved in the white marble interior walls, most notably the circular frieze quotation, "I have sworn upon the altar of God eternal hostility against every form of tyranny over the mind of man." From the front of the memorial you can see the White House directly across the Tidal Basin. The memorial is open 24 hours; rangers are on duty from 8am to midnight.

Continue around the Tidal Basin, heading north on 15th Street (Raoul Wallenberg Place). On your right, you'll pass the Bureau of Engraving and Printing and, farther

An Unequaled Man

In addition to Thomas Jefferson's numerous accomplishments—which included penning the Declaration of Independence and the Statute of Virginia for religious freedom; serving as George Washington's secretary of state, John Adams's vice-president, and America's third president; and founding the University of Virginia—he was an expert in such diverse fields as law, music, agriculture, history, architecture, astronomy, and anthropology. President John F. Kennedy, toasting a group of 29 Nobel Prize winners at a dinner in 1962, told his guests they were "the most extraordinary collection of talent, of human knowledge, that has ever been gathered together at the White House—with the possible exception of when Thomas Jefferson dined alone."

along, the United States Holocaust Memorial Museum, its austere architecture evocative of the bleak Nazi era.

On your left is the:

6. **Washington Monument.** When Pierre Charles L'Enfant planned the city, he chose a site slightly west of this for an equestrian statue of George Washington. (When the equestrian idea was later abandoned in favor of a monolith, it was necessary to select a less marshy spot to support so huge a structure.) Congress authorized the monument in 1783, while Washington was still alive (he personally approved the site), but failed to follow through; the new nation was sorely short of funds. It wasn't until the early 1830s, with the 100th anniversary of Washington's birth approaching, that the Washington National Memorial Society, founded by a group of private citizens, selected a design by eminent architect Robert Mills. His original plan called for a circular colonnaded Greek temple base, a feature later scrapped, once again for lack of money. In 1848 the cornerstone was laid (with the same trowel George Washington had used to lay the Capitol cornerstone) and the obelisk begun. After decades of interruption (partly due to the Civil War, when Monument grounds were used as a stockyard and

slaughterhouse for Union forces), President Grant approved $200,000 in federal monies, and the memorial was finally completed in 1884. It opened to the public in 1888.

At 555 feet 5$\frac{1}{8}$ inches, it is the world's tallest masonry structure. Its marble walls are 15 feet thick at the base and 18 inches at the crown. From the top of the monument (do ascend) you'll enjoy spectacular views of the Capitol and Smithsonian buildings to the east, the gleaming white Jefferson Memorial to the south, the Lincoln and Vietnam memorials to the west, and the White House to the north. Monument grounds are the scene of numerous festivities, ranging from the Smithsonian Kite Festival every March to July 4th concerts and fireworks, and its Sylvan Theatre is the scene of military band concerts on summer evenings.

An interesting note: Between the 1880s and the 1920s, all the land west of the Washington Monument toward the Lincoln Memorial was reclaimed from marsh and swampland. Until then, the Potomac sometimes overflowed as far as the White House lawn.

The Washington Monument is open from the first Sunday in April to Labor Day daily from 8am to midnight; hours are daily from 9am to 5pm the rest of the year. The last elevator goes up 15 minutes prior to closing.

Winding Down Within walking distance of the Washington Monument is the **Old Ebbitt Grill**, 675 15th Street NW, between F and G Streets (tel. 202/347-4801), a reconstruction of a historic 1856 D.C. saloon (presidents from Grant to Harding were patrons). Its interior is gorgeous, with Persian rugs strewn on beautiful oak and marble floors, beveled mirrors, and flickering antique gaslight chandeliers. Seating is in plush velvet banquettes and booths. Though its ambience is ultra-elegant, the Ebbitt's daily menu offers many inexpensive choices—pasta, sandwiches, crabcakes, salads, burgers, omelets, and entrées such as trout parmesan. Everything is delicious, and portions are large. You worked off hundreds of calories traipsing around those monuments; treat yourself to a hot fudge sundae for dessert. The Ebbitt is open almost around the clock.

CAPITOL HILL

Start: The fountain at Bartholdi Park.

Metro: Federal Center SW. There's only one exit, which deposits you at the corner of 3rd and D Streets SW. Cross 3rd Street and follow D to 2nd Street; turn left and walk two blocks to the corner of Independence and Washington Avenues SW, where you'll see a striking fountain. That's your goal.

Finish: Union Station.

Time: At least 4 hours, not counting a lunch break.

Best Times: Start in the morning, take a lunch break, then finish up in the afternoon. Many buildings close at 4:30pm and are also closed on Thanksgiving and Christmas.

Centered around the gleaming and gracefully proportioned white-domed Capitol building that historian Allan Nevins called "the spirit of America in stone," the Capitol Hill area is replete with marble palaces housing the workings of government. Among these noble edifices are the Senate and House office buildings, the Supreme Court, the Library of Congress, and Union Station. In quiet contrast, this is also a residential neighborhood, with neat tree-lined streets of 19th-century townhouses. The hill itself, originally the site of Native American encampments, was called Jenkins Hill in 1791, when Pierre Charles L'Enfant surveyed the city and declared it "a pedestal waiting for a monument." The Capitol building faces southeast, because L'Enfant and the founding fathers erroneously expected the city would develop in that direction, toward the navigable Anacostia River. When railroads rendered water routes less valuable for transportation, the city developed in a northwest direction instead.

• • • • • • • • • • • • • • • • •

Begin your explorations at the delightful, flower-filled:

1. **Bartholdi Park,** about the size of a city block and part of the U.S. Botanical Garden. Its 30-foot-high cast-iron "fountain of light and water," at the corner of First Street and Independence Avenue SW, was created by French sculptor Frédéric Auguste Bartholdi (1834–1904) for the 1876 International Exposition in Philadelphia. (Bartholdi is, of course, most famous for his Statue of Liberty in New York Harbor). Originally lit by 12 gaslights, the fountain has been illuminated by electric globes since 1915. Three classical bronze *nereids* (sea nymphs)—clad in headdresses of leaves and clinging drapery clasped by scallop shells at the waist—support the basin, while water-spouting sea monsters, shells, and fish encircle its base at their feet. The fountain is crowned by three kneeling young tritons (sea gods) catching water in seaweed. When the Exposition closed, at the suggestion of landscape architect Frederick Law Olmsted the U.S. government purchased the fountain from Bartholdi and placed it in the Botanic Garden, which, at that time, was in the center of the Mall. It was moved to this location in 1932. Stroll about the flower gardens here; petunias, sunflowers, lilies, morning glories, roses, zinnias, cosmos, and phlox bloom amid tall ornamental grasses, and benches are sheltered by vine-covered bowers. There's also a touch and fragrance garden containing herbs such as pineapple-scented sage.

Across Independence Avenue is the main building of the:

2. **United States Botanic Garden,** first proposed by George Washington, and enthusiastically supported by Jefferson and Madison; it opened on the Mall in 1820. The Conservatory, built between 1931 and 1933 along the lines of a 17th-century French orangerie, is entered via a room with two reflecting pool fountains under a skylight. Within are

Capitol Hill

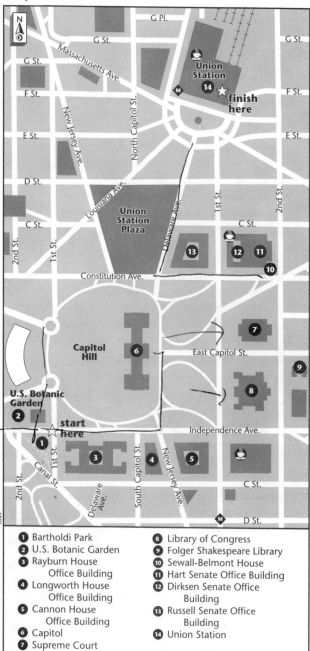

1. Bartholdi Park
2. U.S. Botanic Garden
3. Rayburn House
    Office Building
4. Longworth House
    Office Building
5. Cannon House
    Office Building
6. Capitol
7. Supreme Court
8. Library of Congress
9. Folger Shakespeare Library
10. Sewall-Belmont House
11. Hart Senate Office Building
12. Dirksen Senate Office
    Building
13. Russell Senate Office
    Building
14. Union Station

collections of plants from subtropical, tropical, and desert regions, ranging from dense jungle areas with tranquil lotus pools to cactus gardens. Orchids are in brilliant bloom the year round. Benches in shady corners create the illusion of a carefully tended woods. Surrounding the building on three sides is a flagstone terrace. Spring through fall it is graced by white canvas umbrella tables, each set in an intimate outdoor nook enclosed by trellises and planters. The terrace is the scene of changing floral displays, often with musical accompaniment—for instance, an ikebana show might be enhanced by Japanese flute music. In the planning stages at this writing is the adjacent three-acre National Garden, which will include an Environmental Learning Center with interactive exhibits, a rose garden showcasing over 200 varieties, a regional plant collection, and a water garden that will be dedicated to the First Ladies of the United States. The USBG is open daily from 9am to 5pm.

Upon exiting the Botanical Garden, walk to First Street and Independence Avenue; turn left on Independence. You'll pass three House of Representatives' office buildings. The first, on the corner, is the immense:

3. **Rayburn House Office Building,** its Ionic-columned entrance flanked by two seated statues representing the *Majesty of the Law* (a stern male figure holding a sword) and the *Spirit of Justice* (a torch-bearing female figure with a child at her knee). The building fills the entire block between First and South Capitol Streets.

Next to it, between South Capitol Streeet and New Jersey Avenue, is the:

4. **Longworth House Office Building,** another imposing neoclassical structure with an upper-level Ionic colonnade. Beyond it is the striking:

5. **Cannon House Office Building,** with an entry diagonal to the corner. On the other side of the Capitol stands this building's twin, the Russell Senate Office Building. You can visit your congressperson in one of the three buildings. Just ask at the reception area in any building for a list of their names and the location of their offices. All four of these congressional office buildings can be reached by a private subway that travels through the bowels of the:

6. **Capitol,** towering above you to the north across Independence Avenue. George Washington himself laid the cornerstone in 1793. He was also on the committee that chose architect William Thornton's design for the building, for its "grandeur . . . simplicity . . . and beauty." The Capitol dome is one of the largest in the world, weighing in at nine million pounds. The bronze female figure of *Freedom* crowning the dome was created by Thomas Crawford, an American sculptor working in Italy; it weighs 14,985 pounds and stands 19$^{1}/_{2}$ feet tall. Crawford also created the bas reliefs in the pediments above the Corinthian-columned main entrance and at the entrance to the U.S. Senate (to the right of the dome as you face it); they are *Genius of America* and *Progress of Civilization,* respectively.

The Capitol has been expanded over the years, and the only part of the original building that can be seen is the west front. To tour the building, you enter from the east front into the Rotunda, where tours leave every 15 minutes. If there's a long line, you may have to wait, although you're perfectly free to wander around the Capitol on your own.

In the **National Statuary Hall** stand 38 of the Capitol's 95 statues of famous Americans, 2 from each state (5 are still forthcoming). Among them are Ethan Allen from Vermont, Henry Clay from Kentucky, Daniel Webster from New Hampshire, and William Jennings Bryan from Nebraska. The hall can only showcase a limited number of statues because of the weight of each one—2,000 pounds.

This room served as the original House of Representatives when there were only 32 states. The curved ceiling fills it with echoes; if you stand on a designated spot on one side you can whisper and still be heard at a spot on the other side. John Quincy Adams, a former president who later served nine terms as a congressman, had a cerebral stroke while giving a speech on this floor and died two days later.

Downstairs is a fascinating room filled with exhibits about the building and its builders. Called the **"Crypt,"** it was originally built as a tomb for George and Martha Washington, who preferred to be interred at Mount Vernon. The still-empty tomb is directly below where you are standing and is used to store the catafalque on which the nation's heroes lie in state in the Rotunda. Nine presidents have lain in state in the Capitol, starting with Abraham Lincoln and including John F. Kennedy and Lyndon Johnson.

In the Crypt, note the large sculpture of Abraham Lincoln by Gutzon Borglum, who designed Mount Rushmore; if you look closely, you may notice that one side of his face looks more haggard than the other. This was done to illustrate the toll the presidency took on Lincoln; the artist's omission of Lincoln's left ear denotes his incomplete life, cut short by his assassination. Another statue by Adelaide Johnson pays homage to three pioneers of women's suffrage: Lucretia Mott, Elizabeth Cady Stanton, and Susan B. Anthony. To learn about them and other early feminists, visit the nearby Sewall-Belmont House (see Stop 10, below).

There's a real treasure on this level: the **old Supreme Court chamber,** in use from 1810 to 1860. The first permanent meeting place of the court has been fully restored, down to the quill pens and the hooks for the justices' robes. During much of this period, the court was presided over by John Marshall, who was known as the Great Chief Justice, a man of the people, an aristocrat in muddy boots and torn britches. Directly upstairs is the re-created old Senate Chamber, used from 1810 to 1859 (the furniture is reproduction, except for the vice president's desk), where Daniel Webster, Henry Clay, and John C. Calhoun moved fellow senators with their oratory. When the Senate moved out, the Supreme Court moved upstairs and met here until 1935, when it moved to the marble temple across the street.

On the third floor of the Capitol are the current **Senate and House of Representative chambers.** You may visit both. If they are in session, you must first obtain a pass from the office of your senator or representative; check their whereabouts at the reception area of any of the Senate or House office buildings on either side of the Capitol.

The House of Representatives, the largest legislative chamber in the world, has walnut paneling with pilasters of gray marble; the representatives sat at desks until 1913, but now they sit on benches. It is said that there are blood stains on the stairs leading to the reporters' gallery in the House, a remnant of an 1890 incident in which Congressman

William Taulbee of Kentucky was shot and killed by a reporter, Charles Kincaid, of the *Louisville Times,* after he criticized an article Kincaid had written. (The journalist was acquitted.)

In the Senate chamber, on the other side of this floor, members sit at the original desks made in 1819. In niches below the ceiling are busts of the first 20 presidents of the United States. After the 1992 elections brought the number of female senators to six, a new senators-only women's restroom was installed—a sign that women have finally arrived in the halls of power.

Legend has it that a cat appears in the catafalque of the Capitol on the eve of the changing of an administration or before a national tragedy.

Take a Break In the Capitol complex, your best bet for lunch is the low-priced buffet in the **Dirksen Senate Office Building South Buffet Room,** 1st and C Streets, Monday through Friday between 11:30am and 2:30pm, in an attractive marble-colonnaded art deco dining room furnished with comfortable leather chairs and white-linened tables, you can help yourself to unlimited viands from the carvery station, about eight additional hot entrées, rice/potato/pasta dishes, vegetables, a fruit and salad bar, a make-your-own-sundae bar, and beverages.

To get to the Buffet Room, take the free subway that runs through the underbelly of the Capitol (a bit of an adventure in itself); ask Capitol Police for directions. Or, wait until Stop 12, when you will be right at this building.

Upon leaving the Capitol, walk straight ahead through Capitol grounds (on East Capitol Street). Just across First Street, to your left, is the:

7. **Supreme Court.** This gleaming marble palace of justice is the highest court in the land. Its classical grandeur is reinforced by the pledge over the Corinthian-columned entrance: "Equal Justice Under Law." So majestic is the neoclassical temple created by architect Cass Gilbert that when it became the court's home in 1935, one justice remarked, "We will look like nine black beetles in the Temple of Karnak"; another suggested that he and his colleagues

ought to enter such pompous precincts on elephants. However, I tend to agree with Chief Justice Charles Evans Hughes' assessment at the cornerstone-laying ceremony: "The Republic endures and this is the symbol of its faith."

The Supreme Court is charged with deciding whether actions of Congress, the president, the states, and lower courts are in accord with the Constitution, and with interpreting that document's enduring principles and applying them to new situations and changing conditions. The Court's rulings are final, reversible only by another Supreme Court decision, or, in some cases, by an Act of Congress or Constitutional amendment. Some 6,500 petitions from lower courts are brought to the Supreme Court each year. Only about 120 of these are subsequently chosen for review, usually those of national or constitutional relevance or cases that have drawn opposing views in lower courts. Four of the nine justices must want to review a particular case before it can be brought before the court.

The courtroom itself is upstairs. Visitors may enter, although seating is limited. The justices hear cases October through late April, Monday through Wednesday between 10am and 3pm, with a lunch hour from noon to 1pm. Sessions alternate in approximately two-week intervals between sittings to hear cases and deliver opinions and recesses for consideration of business before the court. Check the *Washington Post*'s "Supreme Court Calendar" to find out what cases are on the docket the day of your tour. When the Court is not in session, every hour on the half-hour between 9:30am and 3:30pm you can attend a free lecture about Court procedure in the courtroom. Or you can go downstairs and see a 20-minute film on the workings of the Court. While you're down here, note the grand spiral staircases, which are similar to those at the Vatican and the Paris Opéra Granier.

When you leave the Supreme Court, turn left and walk a block to the:

8. **Library of Congress,** First Street SE, between Independence Avenue and East Capitol Street. The nation's library was established in 1800 "for the purchase of such books as may be necessary for the use of Congress"; its concept has been infinitely expanded in subsequent years. It is

today the largest library in the world, housing more than 27 million books in all languages (only about a third of the collection is in English), 540 miles of shelves, and 22 reading rooms. At this writing—and all statistics listed here are changing even as I write—the collection includes more than 101 million items, with new materials being acquired at the rate of 10 items per minute! In its capacity as issuer of copyrights (since 1870) the Library of Congress receives two copies of every book printed in the United States. Even the staff of 5,000 cannot catalogue articles as fast as they come in.

The Library of Congress's original collection of books was destroyed when the British burned the Capitol (where it was then housed) during the War of 1812. Thomas Jefferson then sold the institution his eclectic personal library of 6,487 books as a replacement for $23,950; this became the nucleus of the vast repository. Jefferson—who early on envisioned the library's eventual unlimited scope—believed there was "no subject to which a Member of Congress may not have occasion to refer."

The institution consists of three immense buildings connected by a series of underground tunnels. The first you'll come to—and by far the most impressive—is the magnificent Italian Renaissance–style **Thomas Jefferson Building,** which opened in 1897, when horse-drawn wagons moved 800 tons of materials from the Capitol to the library's new precincts. Its sumptuous design was meant to establish America as a cultured nation with institutions of awe-inspiring grandeur equal to any in Europe. Dozens of American painters and sculptors worked for eight years on its lavish interior, which includes ornate floor mosaics, over 100 murals, 42 sculptures, overhead vaults embellished with allegorical paintings, and bas reliefs, not to mention ornamental cornucopias, ribbons, vines, and garlands. Three massive bronze doors at the main entrance represent Tradition, Writing, and Printing.

The Main Reading Room, under a 160-foot, 23-carat gilded dome, has terra-cotta walls and tricolor columns composed of creamy Italian marble, rosy Algerian marble, and gray marble from Tennessee. The columns are capped by female figures representing art, commerce, religion, law, poetry, and philosophy, and flanked by statues of Shakespeare, Homer, Bacon, Beethoven, Newton, and Moses. The painting beneath the cupola depicts the evolution of knowledge in the western world. It was originally assumed that the Jefferson Building would suffice for 150 years of collecting; in fact, it filled up in 13.

In 1939, it was supplemented by the **John Adams Building,** a much more simple classical–art deco structure faced with Georgia white marble. Though named for Adams, it, too, honors Jefferson, with panels in the South Reading Room inscribed with quotations from his writing, such as:

Educate and inform the mass of the people. Enable them to see that it is their interest to preserve peace and order, and they will preserve them. Enlighten the people generally, and tyranny and oppression of the body and mind will vanish like evil spirits at the dawn of day.

A third repository—the **James Madison Memorial Building,** named for the father of the Constitution and the Bill of Rights—was completed in 1981. Along with the Federal Bureau of Investigation (FBI) and the Pentagon, it is one of the three largest buildings in the Washington area. In 1783, Madison was the first sponsor of the idea of a library for Congress, and he proposed a list of books for it that would be useful to legislators. Madison quotations flank the main entrance on Independence Avenue. To the left:

Knowledge will forever govern ignorance; and a people who mean to be their own governours, must arm themselves with the power which knowledge gives.

And to the right:

What spectacle can be more edifying or more seasonable, than that of liberty and learning, each leaning on the other for their mutual and surest support?

Tours depart Monday through Friday at 10am, 1pm, and 3pm from the lobby of the James Madison Building, 101 Independence Avenue SE. I suggest coming back another time to take one. Less time consuming is a 22-minute slide presentation called *America's Library;* it's shown weekdays every half hour from 9am to a half hour

The Library of Congress: The "Nation's Attic"

Just what is filling up building after building of the Library of Congress? A complete list could comprise an entire book, but the following will give you some idea of the scope of this vast and eclectic collection:

- The world's largest cartographic collection—more than four million maps and atlases, some of them dating back to the mid-14th century.
- Major collections of 18th-century American newspapers.
- Nine million photographs and negatives, including original prints by many noted photographers.
- Rare Stradivarius violins, violas, and cellos.
- A 1455 copy of the Gutenberg bible, the first book made with moveable type (one of three perfect copies in existence, it's one of the world's most valuable books).
- The largest collection of incunabula (books printed before 1500) in the Western Hemisphere.
- Close to 700,000 motion-picture reels, among them the earliest motion-picture print made by Thomas Edison in 1893.
- Thomas Jefferson's rough draft of the Declaration of Independence.
- Transcription discs for thousands of hours of radio programming, beginning in 1926.
- More than 3 1/2 million pieces of music.
- The magic books of Harry Houdini.
- Over 80,000 volumes of Russian literature.
- Two drafts of Lincoln's Gettysburg Address.
- A valuable collection of prints and sketches by James Whistler.
- The papers of Sigmund Freud, many presidents, Alexander Graham Bell, Orville and Wilbur Wright, and others.
- The contents of Lincoln's pockets on the night he was shot.
- Over 1.3 million recordings of music and the spoken word, ranging from a recording of the voice of Kaiser Wilhelm II to modern CDs.

before closing. To get to the Madison Building, walk the length of the block, cross Independence Avenue, and turn left.

☕ **Take a Break**   The **James Madison Memorial Building of the Library of Congress,** 101 Independence Avenue SE, houses an elegant **sixth-floor cafeteria** with a windowed wall offering panoramic city views. The food here is fresh, homemade, and inexpensive. Lunch is served Monday through Friday between 12:30 and 2pm, with lighter fare available through 3:30pm. Or, you can opt for the very reasonably priced prix-fixe lunch served weekdays from 11:30am to 2pm in the adjacent, and even more elegant, **Montpelier Room.** Menus change daily; a typical meal here might begin with cream of broccoli soup, followed by prime rib, lyonnaise potatoes, honeyed carrots, salad bar selections, bread and butter, and beverage.

Walk back on First Street past the Thomas Jefferson Building, making a right at East Capitol Street. Cross Second Street. On your right is the:

9. **Folger Shakespeare Library,** built in 1930. Dwarfed by the imposing Supreme Court and Library of Congress, the compact Folger still manages to hold its own on Capitol Hill. Its neoclassical Georgian marble facade is decorated with nine bas-relief scenes from Shakespeare's plays. A statue of Puck stands in the west garden, and quotations from the Bard and contemporaries such as Ben Jonson enhance its exterior walls. An Elizabethan garden on the east side of the building is planted with period flowers and herbs, many of which are mentioned in Shakespeare's works. The Library was founded by ardent collectors Henry Clay Folger, a career executive with Standard Oil, and his wife, Emily, who together amassed the world's largest collection of Shakespeare's printed works. An important research center not only for Shakespearean scholars but for students of the Renaissance, the library has grown to comprise some 250,000 books, 100,000 of them rare. Walk into the oak-paneled Great Hall, reminiscent of a Tudor long gallery, to see exhibits from the permanent collection—costumes, Renaissance musical instruments, playbills, and more. At the far end of the Great Hall is an Elizabethan innyard theater used for concerts and Shakespeare-related events.

From the Folger Shakespeare Library, cross East Capitol Street and follow Second Street, walking behind the

Supreme Court to Constitution Avenue NE, where you'll see a red brick house (no. 144) with dormer windows and a double stairway leading up to the front door. It's the:

10. **Sewall-Belmont House,** a rich repository of suffragist and feminist history. The entrance is on the second floor. This Federal/Queen Anne–style house, open to the public, was once the home of Alice Paul (1885–1977), who founded the National Woman's Party (NWP) in 1913 and wrote the original Equal Rights Amendment to the Constitution. Paul, who held three law degrees and a Ph.D. in sociology, was jailed seven times in the United States and Great Britain for the cause of women's suffrage. She lived here from 1929 to 1972. In 1978, ownership of the house was transferred to the Woman's Party Corporation, and NWP offices were installed on the ground floor. NWP members have included Katharine Hepburn, Gloria Swanson, Margaret Mead, Mary Pickford, and Georgia O'Keeffe.

The house itself is one of the oldest in the Washington area, with one part dating from 1680. Robert Sewall built the present house in 1800, incorporating the earlier structure into it. Albert Gallatin, secretary of the treasury under Madison and Jefferson (he arranged the financing of the Louisiana Purchase, which doubled the size of the United States), rented the house from 1803 to 1813; during that time, he was visited here by both presidents. The house suffered some damage when the British set fire to it during the War of 1812. It remained in the Sewall family for 123 years. The Belmont in the house name is for Alva Belmont, who was once married to Cornelius Vanderbilt II; she was a major benefactor of the NWP.

The drawing room to the right as you enter, and the parlor across the hall from it, have silver-hinged doors from Daniel Webster's home; and many gilt-framed mirrors in the house were acquired from the French embassy. Rooms are adorned with portraits and busts of women who were active in the suffrage and equal rights movements, including Susan B. Anthony, Lucretia Mott, Elizabeth Cady Stanton, and Alice Paul herself. Also on view are Edith Ogden Heidel's statue *Thinking Woman,* a feminist version of Rodin's *The Thinker;* a small sculpture of Sybil Ludington, a Revolutionary War heroine who made a ride reminiscent of Paul Revere's legendary one (only hers was four times longer); an exquisite ivory and marble life-size statue of Joan of Arc (a replica of one in the cathedral at Reims); a four-piece silver serving set that belonged to Clara Barton; and Susan B. Anthony's rolltop desk. Upstairs, in Alice Paul's bedroom, you can see historic photographs relating to the NWP. Also take a look at the Congressional Room, where women used to stay when they came to town to lobby Congress for equal rights. Admission is free; donations are appreciated. Docent tours are given throughout the day on request. The house is open Tuesday through Friday from 10am to 3pm, Saturday from noon to 4pm, Sunday from noon to 4pm March through October only.

On leaving the Sewall-Belmont House, walk right on Constitution Avenue to the Senate office buildings. The first you'll pass, which warrants a look inside, is the modern:

11. **Hart Senate Office Building,** named for Michigan Senator Philip Aloysius Hart. In its atrium is a massive Alexander Calder sculpture called *Mountains and Clouds,* the only Calder work to combine a stationary sculpture with a mobile. The artist created the model in 1976, the last year of his life, and the sculpture was installed posthumously.

Connected to the Hart Building via a walkway adjacent to the Calder is the:

12. **Dirksen Senate Office Building,** built in 1956 and named after Illinois Senator Everett McKinley Dirksen. Walk back out on the street to see its facade, which features motifs of laborers. Extra-long windows give the impression that it has only four very tall floors, though there are actually eight.

Cross First Avenue and continue on Constitution Avenue to Delaware Avenue, where you'll see the main entrance to the impressive neoclassic:

13. **Russell Senate Office Building,** the mirror image of the Cannon Building, the House of Representatives' office building directly opposite it on the other side of the Capitol. Walk in to see the gorgeous rotunda and circular Corinthian colonnade on the second level. You can visit your state senator in one of these buildings. Just ask at the

reception area in any of them for a list of the senators with the location of their offices.

Turn right on Delaware Avenue. You'll pass a park called Union Station Plaza as you make your way to:

14) **Union Station,** a stunning beaux-arts monument to the great age of rail travel, and one of the most aesthetically nurturing architectural interiors I have ever experienced. Built between 1903 and 1907, it was designed by noted architect Daniel Burnham, who, as a member of the illustrious McMillan Commission assembled in 1900 to beautify the city in a manner befitting an important world capital, counseled, "Make no little plans. They have no magic to stir men's blood. . . ." Union Station, one of the commission's "big plans" (at its opening the largest train station in the world), was modeled after the Baths of Diocletian and the Arch of Constantine in Rome. It's fronted by a replica of the Liberty Bell and Laredo Taft's monumental fountain, which depicts Christopher Columbus flanked by figures representing the Old and New Worlds he brought together (Taft also created the pediment above the entry to the House of Representatives). Over 100 eagles are portrayed in the facade. The central entrance has six massive Ionic columns topped by allegorical figures representing Fire, Electricity, Freedom, Imagination, Agriculture, and Mechanics.

The **Main Hall,** entered via graceful 50-foot Constantinian arches, is simply awe-inspiring. Under a nine-story barrel-vaulted ceiling inlaid with 22-carat gold-leaf, it has acres of white marble flooring punctuated by red Champlain dots, bronze grilles, and rich Honduran mahogany paneling. Its balcony is adorned with 36 sculptures of Roman legionnaires. (Originally, the legionnaires were naked, though not anatomically correct; the wife of a railroad president complained and shields were added.) A central elliptical mahogany kiosk, inspired by a Renaissance baldacchino, contains a bilevel café and a visitor information center. The adjacent **East Hall** has scagliola marble walls and columns, a gorgeous hand-stenciled skylight ceiling, and stunning murals inspired by ancient Pompeiian art. In the 1940s and 1950s the East Hall was home to the elegant Savarin restaurant, which was, at the time, the only integrated restaurant in Washington. Today it's the station's most plush shopping venue.

In the heyday of rail travel, many important events took place at Union Station. Visiting royalty and heads of state were greeted in the lavish Presidential Suite adjoining the East Hall; today it's a restaurant. General Pershing was welcomed by President Woodrow Wilson upon his return from France. South Pole explorer Rear Admiral Byrd was also feted at Union Station on his homecoming. And Franklin Delano Roosevelt's funeral train, bearing his casket, was met here by thousands of mourners in 1945. But with the decline of rail travel, the station fell into disrepair. Rain damage caused part of the roof to cave in, and the entire building was sealed for public safety in 1981. That same year, Congress enacted legislation to preserve and faithfully restore this national treasure. Following a $150-million renovation, it reopened in 1988.

Today Union Station is once again a vibrant "temple of transport," exquisitely restored and gleaming, with 100 retail shops, restaurants, a food court, and a nine-screen cinema complex. It is moving to remember Burnham's own unwittingly prophetic words: ". . . a noble, logical diagram once recorded will never die, but long after we are gone will be a living thing, asserting itself with ever-growing insistency. Let your watchword be order and your beacon beauty."

 Winding Down　There are many eating places in the station, and you might wish to peruse them all before making a choice. One of my favorites is **America,** with seating on three levels and café tables sprawling out into the Main Hall. Its art deco interior includes large murals and paintings ranging in subject matter from the American West to a whimsical depiction of astronauts and superheroes in outer space. A vast menu offers reasonably priced American classics—meatloaf with mashed potatoes, baked macaroni and cheese, roast turkey with stuffing and giblet gravy, and sandwiches ranging from New Orleans fried oyster po'boys to Philadelphia cheese steaks. It's open from 11:30am daily.

The lower-level **Food Court** is another good choice. Though I don't usually like food courts (too big, noisy, and sterile), this one's most attractive, enhanced by oak and pine paneling, subtle lighting, and colorful canvas umbrellas over the tables. The vast space is divided to create intimate dining areas. You can get just about anything here—fresh seafood, sushi, salads, deli sandwiches, tacos, pizzas, falafel, deli, and much, much more.

DUPONT CIRCLE
MUSEUMS

Start: Dupont Circle.

Metro: Dupont Circle, north exit.

Finish: National Geographic Explorers Hall.

Time: Approximately 5 hours, so that you can spend some time in the museums that most interest you.

Best Times: Wednesdays through Saturdays, because all the places featured in the tour are open, unless it happens to be a federal holiday. If you plan your tour for another day, check the schedules of the places you are most interested in visiting so you won't be disappointed. Start out about 12:15pm, since Anderson House (Stop 3), a must-see, doesn't open until 1pm. That will allow you plenty of time to peruse the Phillips Collection (Stop 2), which I highly recommend.

The Dupont Circle area, which centers on the fountained park of that name, is home to some of the city's most interesting museums and historic houses—from the world-class Phillips Collection, a showcase for modern art, to the retirement home of President Woodrow Wilson. At the turn of the century, this section of town was a wealthy enclave, its streets lined with impressive beaux-arts townhouses. Though today the neighborhood's character is vastly changed, the patrician population having moved elsewhere, you'll still see many magnificent mansions along this walk. Architecture aside, Dupont Circle is a vital section of town, housing dozens of chic restaurants, movie theaters, shops, and nightspots. It is also the hub of Washington's gay community.

● ● ● ● ● ● ● ● ● ● ● ● ● ● ● ● ●

Starting Out   Since you're advised to begin this tour shortly after noon, consider a fortifying brunch before starting out. A good choice is **Kramerbooks & Afterwords, A Café,** 1517 Connecticut Avenue NW, between Q Street and Dupont Circle (tel. 202/387-1462). This schmoozy bookstore and moderately priced restaurant is pretty much open around the clock. Your choices here range from breakfasty items to sandwiches, pastas, and salads. Yummy shakes are served here, too, with and without alcohol, and desserts like chocolate fudge cake. There's seating in a glassed-in solarium and at outdoor café tables.

Or walk up a few blocks to the comfortable **Café Petitto,** 1724 Connecticut Avenue NW, between R and S Streets (tel. 202/462-8771). Petitto's sets out lavish prix-fixe antipasto displays daily. These tempting buffets always feature about 50 items—stuffed grape leaves, pasta salads, bean salads, escarole and pancetta, cold cuts, and much more. Great pizzas, pastas, and Italian sandwiches are here, too. It opens daily at 11:30am.

Begin your tour at:

1. **Dupont Circle.** This lively park honoring Civil War hero Navy Rear Admiral Samuel Francis du Pont (1803–65) is a popular rendezvous spot—musicians often perform on warm weekends, occasional demonstrations take place, chess players wax intent over spirited games, and young Washingtonians converge to hang out and bask in the summer sun. The Circle came into being in 1884, when

Congress erected a small bronze equestrian statue here in recognition of du Pont's distinguished service to his country. However, the du Pont family found it unworthy and hired the extremely prestigious team of Daniel Chester French and Henry Bacon (designers of the Lincoln Memorial) to build the grand memorial you see today. The fountain's classical figures, framed by square columns, represent a seafarer's guides—the stars, the sea, and the wind.

From Dupont Circle, walk northeast on Massachusetts Avenue NW and make a right at 21st Street, noting, as you do, the gorgeous Indonesian Embassy at the corner. At Q Street is the:

2. **Phillips Collection of Modern Art,** 1600 21st Street NW, conceived as "a museum of modern art and its sources." The stellar collection of Duncan and Marjorie Phillips, avid proponents of modernism, is housed in an elegant 1890s Georgian Revival mansion that was Duncan Phillips's childhood home. In the main house—where the Phillipses lived until their burgeoning collection totaled 600 pieces—oak-paneled rooms with plush furnishings make an inviting backdrop for viewing art.

Today the collection comprises more than 2,500 works, of which 250 to 300 pieces are on exhibit at any given time. Highlights include works—most of them gems—by Bonnard (the largest collection in North America), van Gogh, Klee, Braque, Matisse, O'Keeffe, Gauguin, Hopper, Cézanne, Monet, Degas, and Picasso, among many others. Ingres, Delacroix, Manet, El Greco, Goya, Corot, Constable, Courbet, Giorgione, and Chardin are among the "sources" or forerunners of modernism represented. An excellent group of abstract expressionist paintings—including a roomful of Rothkos—occupies the first floor. Curatorial wisdom has placed related works near one another. For instance, paintings by Richard Deibenkorn are near a Matisse—the latter was a major influence on the former. Impressionists dominate the second floor, where comfortable armchairs are set up for viewing Renoir's *Luncheon of the Boating Party,* a cornerstone of the collection. Do note *The Blue Room,* which Picasso painted at age 20; its openness, verve, and force show all the promise of his future greatness. Also of interest on this floor is a room of

Dupont Circle Museums

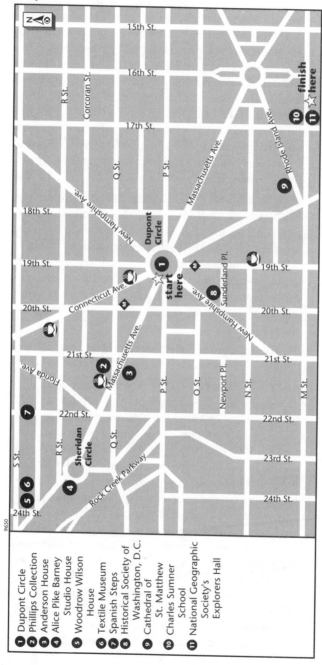

N

15th St.

16th St.

Corcoran St.

17th St.

R St.

Q St.

P St.

New Hampshire Ave.

Massachusetts Ave.

Rhode Island Ave.

finish here ☆

⑩ ⑪

⑨

18th St.

Dupont Circle

19th St.

Connecticut Ave.

①

☆ **start here**

M

⑧

Sunderland Pl.

19th St.

20th St.

M

New Hampshire Ave.

20th St.

21st St.

②

③

Massachusetts Ave.

Florida Ave.

P St.

O St.

Newport Pl.

N St.

21st St.

M St.

⑦

22nd St.

22nd St.

R St.

Sheridan Circle

Q St.

23rd St.

⑤ ⑥

④

Rock Creek Parkway

24th St.

S St.

24th St.

9650

① Dupont Circle
② Phillips Collection
③ Anderson House
④ Alice Pike Barney
   Studio House
⑤ Woodrow Wilson
   House
⑥ Textile Museum
⑦ Spanish Steps
⑧ Historical Society of
   Washington, D.C.
⑨ Cathedral of
   St. Matthew
⑩ Charles Sumner
   School
⑪ National Geographic
   Society's
   Explorers Hall

paintings by Marjorie Phillips. From the second floor, walk through to the main building (the original house) and downstairs to the stunning Jacobean-style music room with parquet floors, rich carved-oak paneling, and an intricate plasterwork ceiling; it is hung, rather incongruously, with cubist paintings by Braque and Picasso. On the second floor of the main house, don't miss the room containing seven charming Paul Klees.

The Phillips is open Monday through Saturday from 10am to 5pm, Sunday noon to 7pm. Admission is charged. Plan to spend at least a half hour to an hour perusing this thrilling collection.

Take a Break   A lovely little **café** on the lower level of the Phillips Collection serves excellent sandwiches, salads, and desserts. Everything is made fresh daily on the premises. Wine and beer are available, and classical music (sometimes light jazz) enhances the ambience. It's open Tuesday through Saturday from 10:45am to 4:30pm, Sunday from noon to 6pm. You don't have to pay museum admission to eat here; there's a separate entrance off the street.

From the Phillips Collection, cross Q Street and Massachusetts Avenue to:

3. **Anderson House,** at 2118 Massachusetts Avenue, adjacent to the Ritz-Carlton Hotel. This limestone-veneered Italianate mansion (more like a palace, really), fronted by twin arches and a Corinthian-columned portico, was built between 1902 and 1905. Pierre Charles L'Enfant, who designed the city of Washington, created the pediment over the mansion's portico. Seventeen varieties of marble were used in the floor and other interior embellishments. Its original owners were career diplomat Larz Anderson III, who served as ambassador to Japan in 1912 and 1913, and his heiress wife, Isabel. Many of the furnishings and objets d'art the Andersons picked up during their extensive travels are displayed here. They include, among many others, Belgian tapestries woven for Louis XIII, 18th-century Louis XV chairs from Versailles, 18th-century Flemish silk tapestries, Revolutionary War swords worn by famous commanders, a Meissen clock and candelabra, 16th-century Spanish wood

carvings, Ming Dynasty jade trees, and a Japanese samurai sword with a carved ivory scabbard.

After Larz's death in 1937, Mrs. Anderson donated the house as headquarters for the Society of the Cincinnati, an organization founded in 1783 for descendants of army officers who fought in the Revolutionary War. (It is named for Cincinnatus, a Roman patriot.) Anderson's great grandfather was a founder, and George Washington was the society's first president-general. Walk to the Great Hall and climb the large stairway to your right, passing a painting on the landing by Jose Villegas y Cordero, one-time director of the Prado in Madrid; it's titled *The Triumph of the Dogaressa Anna Maria Foscari in the Year 1424.* In the Key Room, at the head of the stairs, note the mazelike floor design of sienna and white marble and the displays of Japanese and Chinese lacquers. A mural here shows Larz Anderson's great-grandfather looking on as Lafayette receives his certificate of membership in the Society. The Long Gallery houses museum-like displays, including many of the above-mentioned Asian and European paintings and antiquities. There are ornate Louis XV–style French and English parlors, the ceilings and walls of the former covered in 23-carat gold leaf. In the marble-floored dining room, portraits of the Andersons flank the windows; the custom-made table seats 40. The Anderson's silver, china, and crystal are displayed in the adjoining pantry. Go down the stairway at the end of the Long Gallery, which is lined with portraits of the Society's past president-generals, to check out the ballroom, with massive crystal chandeliers suspended from a 30-foot coffered ceiling, rococo marble columns, and bronze Chinese buddhas in oval niches. The room is modeled on one in Wilton, England designed by famed 17th-century architect Inigo Jones. Also on this floor are the library, the solarium, the breakfast room, and the oak-paneled billiard room, the latter used today for changing art exhibitions. Be sure to peek out a window at the beautiful garden. Anderson House is open to the public Tuesday through Saturday from 1 to 4pm.

From here, continue walking up Massachusetts Avenue, pausing at Sheridan Circle, which centers on an impressive equestrian statue of Civil War Gen. Philip H. Sheridan by

Gutzon Borglum (who is better known for his Mount Rushmore busts of presidents). The Circle is surrounded by magnificent embassy buildings that you'll explore in depth on Walking Tour 6, "Embassy Row." To your left, just above the Circle, look for the stucco facade of the:

4. **Alice Pike Barney Studio House,** 2306 Massachusetts Avenue, built in 1902. Alice Pike Barney, Washington's answer to Gertrude Stein, was a wealthy matron and prominent society leader who owned the house and turned it into a salon in the early 20th century. Barney was also a painter who had studied with Whistler in Paris, and once had a one-woman show at the Corcoran Gallery of Art. This house was the setting for many artistic gatherings in the city, and according to *Washington Society* magazine, was the "meeting place for wit and wisdom, genius and talent, which fine material is leavened by fashionable folk, who would like to be a bit Bohemian if they only knew how." The house, along with family furnishings and memorabilia, was given to the Smithsonian Institution by Mrs. Barney's daughters. It is now in great need of restoration, and hopefully will reopen to the public in the future.

Continue up Massachusetts Avenue to 24th Street and turn right; walk one block to S Street, turn right again, and walk midway up the block to where, on your right, the American flag is flying. This is the:

5. **Woodrow Wilson House,** 2340 S Street NW. When President Woodrow Wilson's second term of office ended in 1921, he and his wife, Edith, moved into this Georgian Revival–style house that she described as "an unpretentious, comfortable, dignified house, suited to the needs of a gentleman's home." Wilson wished to live in Washington to be near the Library of Congress for research purposes. Unfortunately, he was already in bad health when he moved in, and he died almost four years later, at age 68. Mrs. Wilson, 16 years Wilson's junior, continued to live here until her death at age 90. In her will, she bequeathed the house and the personal and political memorabilia in it to the National Trust for Historic Preservation.

In the library you'll see Wilson's movie projector (he was a film buff and local theaters often lent him movies for

Woodrow Wilson: Scholar, Statesman, Idealist

Woodrow Wilson, 28th president of the United States, was born in 1856 in Staunton, Virginia. Reared as a staunch moralist and idealist by his Presbyterian family, Wilson studied history and political science at Princeton and Johns Hopkins, receiving his Ph.D. from the latter. He later taught and served as president at Princeton. He was elected governor of New Jersey in 1910, three years before he assumed the nation's presidency.

Supported in his first term by a Democratic majority in Congress, his administration initiated graduated federal income tax, the Federal Trade Commission to prohibit unfair business practices, and child labor laws. Later legislation included the 18th and 19th constitutional amendments establishing Prohibition and women's voting rights. During his tenure, Wilson refused to invite guests to the White House to further his political agendas, declaring, "I will not permit my home to be used for political purposes." After his first wife, Ellen, died in 1914, Wilson married Edith Bolling Galt.

A proponent of isolationist neutrality in World War I, Wilson was finally forced to declare war on Germany in 1917 in order to make the world "safe for democracy." After the war, he urged a peace of reconciliation based on his Fourteen Points, which—with considerable moderation from a now-hostile Republican Congress—formed the basis for the Treaty of Versailles. Most dear to Wilson, the points proposed an association of nations to resolve future conflicts peaceably. The League of Nations was formed; but to Wilson's dismay, the senate voted not to participate, dooming it to irrelevance.

The strain of an unsuccessful nationwide tour promoting U.S. participation in the League of Nations proved too much for Wilson; he suffered a stroke. Edith basically ran the government for the remainder of his term, engendering the same kind of critical vituperation that politically engaged presidents' wives experience today. Though he was awarded the Nobel Peace Prize in 1920, Wilson never recovered from his disappointment over the League of Nations. He died in 1924.

private viewings); a Gobelins tapestry that was a wedding present from the people of France is displayed in the drawing room. You can also view the typical 1920's kitchen, with a coal and gas stove and oven, an oak ice box, and one of the nation's first electric refrigerators. Wilson's ground-floor office, which his family called the "dugout," contains a baseball given to him at an Army-Navy game that he attended with King George of England (the king autographed it). Upstairs, on his bedside table, lies *Imitations of Christ* by Thomas à Kempis. The house was designed by noted Washington architect Waddy Wood. Forty-five-minute tours of its three floors are given throughout the day, and a 25-minute film tells the life story of the nation's 28th president. Admission is charged. Hours are Tuesday through Sunday from 10am to 4pm.

A few doors down, at 2320 S. Street NW, is the:

6. **Textile Museum.** An outstanding collection of rugs and textiles, it started out modestly, with George Hewitt Myers's purchase of an Oriental rug for his dorm room at Yale in 1896. Myers (as in Bristol-Myers) went on to amass Peruvian tunics, Chinese silks, Mexican serapes, Navajo blankets, and Egyptian tapestries. But the highlight of his collection, numbering more than 12,500 textiles and 500 rugs, is the hand-woven Islamic, Tibetan, Chinese, Caucasian, Turkish, and Navajo rugs. Founded in 1925, the museum is housed in two red brick Georgian buildings: one, Myers's former home (no. 2310), designed in 1913 by John Russell Pope of National Gallery fame; and the other, an adjoining 1908 residence (no. 2320), designed by Waddy Wood (also the architect of Woodrow Wilson's and Alice Pike Barney's homes). Photographs and descriptive text enhance the exhibits, and there is a library on the premises with 13,000 books and periodicals relating to textile arts. A well-stocked gift shop offers Indian silk scarves, Bolivian ruapas, Kilim pillows, Bokhara crepe silk ties, Tibetan rug squares, and much more for anyone who loves textile arts and crafts. An additional note: Myers, also a music and theater buff, entertained Tallulah Bankhead, the Alfred Lunts, and Cornelia Otis Skinner in his home. His son-in-law, Hans Kinders, founded the National Symphony Orchestra. The museum is open Monday through Saturday from 10am to 5pm, Sunday from 1 to 5 pm. Admission is by donation.

From here, walk uphill along S Street, past the residence of the Irish ambassador, then downhill past the embassy of the Laos Peoples Democratic Republic. Turn right at 22nd Street; this will lead you to the graceful, curving:

7. **Spanish Steps,** a magical flower-bordered and tree-shaded granite, brick, and concrete stairway built from 1911 to 1912 and crowned with a lion's head fountain. Stop to listen to the birds in this tranquil little oasis.

Walk down the steps and continue on 22nd Street as far as R Street, turn left, continue a couple of blocks to 21st Street, and turn right. You'll pass the Phillips Collection again, then link up with Massachusetts Avenue, where you turn left and walk back to Dupont Circle. When you reach it, walk around to your right as far as New Hampshire Avenue; turn right onto it and walk to 20th Street. The Victorian house on the corner is the:

8. **Historical Society of Washington, D.C.,** in the Heurich Mansion, built from 1892 to 1894 for German-born brewer and real estate magnate Christian Heurich, whose family donated the land for the Kennedy Center. The house is filled with original furnishings and looks much as it did on its completion, with generous gilding, Victorian touches, and lofty 13½-foot-high ceilings and 12-foot-high doors. The exceptional woodwork, particularly the red oak in the dining room, is the handiwork of German-American craftsmen. Mr. Heurich, who died in the house in 1945 at the age of 102, always went out of his way to demonstrate his loyalty to his adoptive country, saying "Germany is my mother but America is my bride." For added proof, he kept an American flag hanging inside the doorway; you'll find one there today.

The mansion has been the home of the Historical Society of Washington, D.C., since the 1950s. The Society, established in 1894 as the Columbia Historical Society (the name changed a few years later), opens the house to the public Wednesday through Saturday from 10am to 4pm. Hour-long tours, given on the hour between noon and 3pm, take visitors through three of the five floors and 16 of the 31 principal rooms (there are 40 rooms in all), focusing on the domestic life of this upper-class household in the late

Victorian era. The garden behind the house is open to the public Monday through Friday from 9am to 5pm; enter it through the gate around the corner on Sunderland Place. Admission is charged for tours. Call 202/785-2068 for details.

From here, walk along Sunderland Place to 19th Street, turn right, continue to M Street, and turn left. Beyond Connecticut Avenue, as you veer left on Rhode Island Avenue, you'll soon see the:

9. **Cathedral of St. Matthew** on your left. John F. Kennedy worshipped here, and, on November 25, 1963, his coffin rested in front of the altar before the procession to Arlington Cemetery. Today an inscription marks the spot where the casket stood. St. Matthew's magnificent dome is modeled on the Cathedral of Santa Maria del Fiore in Florence. Step inside to see the beautiful chapels, mosaics, Corinthian marble columns, and arched coffered ceiling.

Take a Break   You'll pass **Mick's,** 1220 19th Street NW (tel. 202/785-2866), on your way from the Historical Society to St. Matthew. This moderately priced restaurant, part of an Atlanta-based chain, has a handsome Ralph Lauren–style interior, with banquettes upholstered in classic plaids, gilt-framed equestrian prints adorning knotty-pine walls, and tweed carpeting. Mick's creative American menu includes such options as nachos (they're fabulous), fried green tomatoes topped with roasted red pepper sauce and melted Montrachet cheese, hickory-grilled burgers au poivre served with mustard-cognac sauce, or meat loaf with mashed potatoes and mushroom gravy. Scrumptious desserts are served here, too; try the silky smooth chocolate cream pie. Mick's is open Monday through Friday from 11am, Saturday from noon; it's closed on Sundays.

Cross Rhode Island Avenue at 17th Street, noting, on the corner, the **B'nai B'rith Klutznick Museum** on the premises of that organization's international headquarters. Displays within document 20 centuries of Jewish history. Across 17th Street on your right is the:

10. **Charles Sumner School,** 1201 17th Street NW, established in 1866 as a school for African-American children. The present three-story brick building, erected here in 1871, was designed by architect Adolph Cluss, who won a medal for his public school plans and models at the International Exposition in Vienna, Austria, in 1873. The school was named for senator and abolitionist Charles Sumner of Massachusetts. It housed elementary and secondary classrooms, and, in 1877, held the first high school graduation for African Americans in the city. Later it served as one of the normal schools in the District of Columbia, provided the services of a health clinic, and offered adult education classes at night. After a century of operation, the school closed. In 1986, it reopened as a museum, which is open Monday through Friday from 10am to 5pm. The Sumner School is on the National Register of Historic Places.

Continue right on 17th Street. Across M Street is the:

11. **National Geographic Society's Explorers Hall.** The National Geographic Society was formed in 1888 "to further the increase and diffusion of geographic knowledge," and in the Society's **Explorers Hall** dozens of interactive displays do just that. In Geographica, you can touch a tornado, study the origins of humankind, scrutinize the constellations, explore the vast Martian landscape, and visit Earth Station One, an interactive amphitheater that simulates an orbital flight 23,000 miles above earth. There are exhibits on the exploits of underwater explorer Jacques Cousteau and Adm. Robert E. Peary (the first man to reach the North Pole); displays run the gamut from an *Aepyornis maximus* egg from Madagascar's extinct 1,000-pound flightless "elephant bird" to a 3.9-billion-year-old moon rock. The gift shop on the premises sells a wide array of National Geographic publications, maps, and globes. Explorers Hall is open Monday through Saturday from 9am to 5pm, Sunday from 10am to 5pm. Admission is free.

Return to Dupont Circle via Connecticut Avenue, enjoying the shops along the way.

WASHINGTON SCANDALS

Start: Watergate Hotel.

Metro: Foggy Bottom.

Finish: The Supreme Court.

Time: Approximately 3 hours.

Best Times: Anytime.

Ask Americans if they think their elected leaders are by and large a straitlaced, high-minded bunch and you'll get a collective roll of the eyes. The reason, of course, is that scandalous news never stops pouring out of the nation's capital. Politics and dirty deeds seem to be inseparable; Washington lore is rich with stories of politicians arriving here burning with lofty ideals and ambition only to fall prey to one or another of the grubby demons of human nature. And the sins of the government are thrown into spectacular relief by the klieg lights of the capital's scandal press, which makes its living feeding the public's appetite for news from the gutter.

As Mark Twain put it, Washington houses the only "distinctly native American criminal class." In the spirit of that great American curmudgeon, this tour wades through two-hundred-odd years of avarice, lust, and plain idiocy as cause for amusement and stimulus to a healthy skepticism. The framers of our constitution were indeed wise when they labored to build a government that would keep any individual from accruing too much power—as you'll now be reminded, power is often too great a burden for human frailties to bear.

● ● ● ● ● ● ● ● ● ● ● ● ● ● ● ●

Starting Out It seems apt to begin your tour with breakfast or lunch at one of Washington's most infamous scandal sites, the Watergate Hotel. Its offerings, along with options in the adjacent Kennedy Center, are described in detail in Walking Tour 2, "Monuments and Memorials."

From the Foggy Bottom Metro, make a U-turn to your right after exiting the Metro station; walk through a small park to New Hampshire Avenue. Follow it the equivalent of one block, to Virginia Avenue. You'll see the curving facade of the:

1. **Watergate Hotel/Apartment/Office Complex,** 2600 Virginia Avenue. Just after 1am on June 17, 1972, on the sixth floor of the Watergate, a security guard found a taped-over lock on an office door of the Democratic Party's national headquarters. Suspecting foul play, he called the police, who arrived at the scene to find five well-dressed men huddled under the furniture, all wearing rubber gloves and in possession of high-tech spy gear and 32 sequentially numbered $100 bills.

Thus began the Watergate scandal, perhaps the darkest shadow ever cast over the federal government. By the time the details of the "dirty tricks" perpetrated by the Committee to Reelect the President ("CREEP") emerged, 25 members of President Richard Nixon's staff had received jail terms at the hands of Judge "Maximum John" Sirica; Nixon himself, facing sure impeachment for reasons of perjury, obstruction of justice, misuse of federal funds, and politicization of federal agencies, had resigned (on August 9, 1974); and an outraged "throw-the-bums-out" attitude had settled over the nation.

Take a look inside the elegant Watergate Hotel if you feel so moved. Directly across Virginia Avenue is the:

G. Gordon Liddy & the Watergate Follies

The strength of our democracy is in public consensus and the constitutional safeguards that protect the integrity of that consensus; in the early 1970s, Richard Nixon's administration was willing to bypass any number of those safeguards in the name of gaining four more years. As columnist William White wrote, "We know that politics is extremely rough, but most people in it do, at some point, recognize a line, admittedly indefinable, but a line beyond which you just don't go."

G. Gordon Liddy was general counsel to CREEP (Committee to Reelect the President) at a time when the Nixon campaign was muscling major corporations for illegal contributions—and when the unfortunates on Nixon's infamous "enemies list" (ostensible political opponents who ranged from George McGovern to David Brinkley to Tony Randall) were treated as threats to national security and subjected to wiretapping, burglaries, and tax audits. Liddy was only slightly atypical in his belief that the American "fatherland" was smothering in permissive flab; in his eyes all was fair in the war for the soul of the country. He was fond of proving his discipline by holding his hand over an open flame. And when CREEP director Jeb Magruder muttered something about "getting rid" of some "enemy" in Liddy's presence, the good soldier grimly announced to a subordinate "I have been ordered to kill [the 'enemy']" (he was persuaded that wasn't what Magruder had in mind).

Liddy's first proposal to Presidential Counsel John Dean and Attorney General John Mitchell for doing in the Democrats was a wild million-dollar plan that involved kidnapping radical leaders as well as launching a floating whorehouse off Miami Beach in hopes of luring prominent Dems into compromising positions. When Mitchell told him to come back with something more "realistic," the plan to break into and bug the Democratic National Committee's offices in the Watergate Hotel was born. After two botched attempts and one successful entry (on May 27, 1972), Mitchell ordered Liddy to go back for better information. Liddy's team broke in again on June 17, and the rest is history.

A portrait of the burglary, CREEP's other activities, and the remarkable G. Gordon Liddy began to emerge during the Watergate congressional hearings. John Dean testified that an aggrieved Liddy told him after the disastrous break-in that he would never talk and "If anyone wished to shoot him on the street he was ready." An incredulous public was astounded that Liddy's harebrained schemes even reached the President's ears. That this was indeed the case only became fully apparent when Nixon was finally prevailed upon, in August 1974, to release the taped White House conversations between himself and his chief of staff, Bob Haldeman, from June 23, 1972. As George F. Will put it, the tapes were "more of a smoking howitzer than a smoking gun." Here's a portion:

Nixon: Well, who's the ass—that did [authorize the break-in]? Is it Liddy? Is that the fellow? He must be a little nuts.

Haldeman: He is.

Nixon: I mean he just isn't well screwed on, is he? Is that the problem?

Haldeman: No, but he was under pressure, apparently, to get more information, and as he got more pressure, he pushed the people harder to move harder—

Nixon: Pressure from Mitchell?

Haldeman: Apparently.

Nixon: All right, fine, I understand it all. We won't second-guess Mitchell and the rest.

Nixon then went on to agree with Haldeman on a coverup scheme to tell the FBI to "lay off" its investigation of the break-in because any further breaks in the investigation "would be very unfortunate . . . for the country." As the contents of the tapes broke, it was clear that the President himself was complicit in all the "dirty tricks" perpetrated by his staff, complicit in the myriad ways his administration stepped over (one might say obliterated) that "indefinable line." He resigned from office four days later.

2. **Howard Johnson's Hotel** where G. Gordon Liddy hung out to do his share of the dirty work on the Democrats. The former FBI agent and the counsel to CREEP was paid $235,000—in cash—for his Watergate work.

   Now take Virginia Avenue to the traffic light at 25th Street and turn right, following the curve of the sidewalk around to the:

3. **Kennedy Center for the Performing Arts.** Walk inside and to the back of the Grand Foyer, where a large bust of John F. Kennedy (by Robert Berks) faces the Opera House. We now know that JFK, he of the high-minded idealism and inspirational vision of the presidency as a new "Camelot," was less than pure both in his practice of politics and his personal life. His administration engaged in more than the usual amount of skulduggery, from the infamous Bay of Pigs invasion, to the enlistment of the Chicago mob's help during the 1960 elections, to secret assassination plots. "Operation Mongoose," the most notorious of the latter, targeted Cuba's Fidel Castro; various plans (in which the Mafia may also have played a role) to take out the Cuban leader turned on improbable devices such as poisoned pens, LSD-laced cigars, and exploding seashells.

   And then there were the women: Jack Kennedy, like most of the men in his family, was a compulsive philanderer. He and wife Jackie may have looked the perfect couple, but their marriage was termed "an understanding" at best by a family friend. He may have slowed down after a fashion upon becoming president—he reportedly called a friend one day and said, "There are two naked girls in the room but I'm sitting here reading the *Wall Street Journal.* Does that mean I'm getting old?" Jackie took it all with resigned hauteur; upon finding a pair of panties in the White House bed, she turned to her husband and said, "Here, find out who these belong to—they're not my size." He carried on well-documented affairs with such notables as Jayne Mansfield, Kim Novak, Angie Dickinson, and Marilyn Monroe, who, according to columnist Earl Wilson, is supposed to have said after a night with Jack, "Well, I think I made his back feel better." (Monroe was later passed on to

Washington Scandals

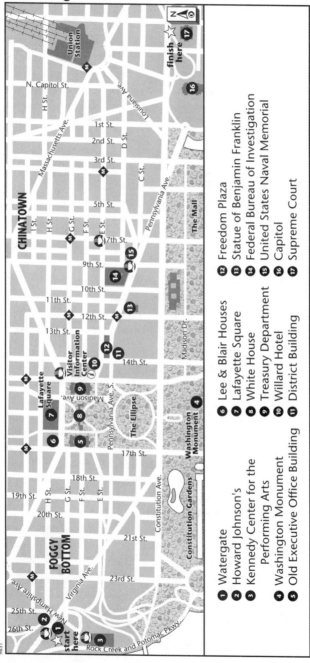

N

start here ☆

finish here ☆

Union Station

CHINATOWN

FOGGY BOTTOM

N. Capitol St.

H St.

Massachusetts Ave.

Louisiana Ave.

1st St.
2nd St.
3rd St.
5th St.
I St.
H St.
G St.
F St.
E St.
7th St.
9th St.
10th St.
11th St.
12th St.
13th St.
14th St.
Visitor Information Center
Lafayette Square
Madison Ave. S.
Pennsylvania Ave. S.
The Ellipse
17th St.
18th St.
19th St.
20th St.
21st St.
23rd St.
25th St.
26th St.
New Hampshire Ave.
Virginia Ave.
H St.
G St.
F St.
E St.
Rock Creek and Potomac Pkwy.
Constitution Ave.
Constitution Gardens
Washington Monument
Madison Dr.
The Mall
Pennsylvania Ave.
C St.
D St.

1 Watergate
2 Howard Johnson's
3 Kennedy Center for the Performing Arts
4 Washington Monument
5 Old Executive Office Building
6 Lee & Blair Houses
7 Lafayette Square
8 White House
9 Treasury Department
10 Willard Hotel
11 District Building
12 Freedom Plaza
13 Statue of Benjamin Franklin
14 Federal Bureau of Investigation
15 United States Naval Memorial
16 Capitol
17 Supreme Court

9651

brother Bobby Kennedy; much as Jack did, Bobby would eventually unceremoniously dump her. Peter Brown and Patte Barham's *Marilyn: The Last Take* (Dutton, 1992) suggests that Monroe's death in 1962 was not a suicide but murder. Fed up with her treatment at the hands of the Kennedys, Monroe had begun to act on threats to go public about her relationships with them. The coroner in the case has said that the Nembutal that killed her could not have been a simple overdose of pills—it was likely administered by injection in a spot unlikely to be discovered during autopsy. Brown and Barham suggest that Bobby Kennedy had something to do with it.)

Another blow to the Kennedy mystique came in 1988 when Judith Campbell Exner, stricken with terminal cancer, decided to clear her conscience. She revealed that during her 2^1/$_2$-year affair with JFK she functioned as courier between the president and the mob, delivering packages and arranging meetings between Kennedy and Chicago Mafia godfather Sam Giancana.

From the rooftop terrace of the Kennedy Center you can see several recognizable Washington landmarks, among them the:

4. **Washington Monument.** Today, even George Washington would not find himself above reproach. Although he married into plenty of money when he took Martha Dandridge Custis to wife (she owned 17,000 acres of land and a Williamsburg townhouse), the general disdained the modest salaries other revolutionary generals earned and accorded himself an expense account of $449,261.50— an emperor's ransom in those days—over his eight years' service. And he reportedly showed the worst possible taste in mistresses, most notably Mary Gibbons, who pumped Washington about his military plans during their trysts and then passed on the information to William Tryon, the royal governor of New York. Tryon capitalized by raiding American seaport towns and destroying much-needed supplies.

Return to Virginia Avenue. Turn right onto it (follow the pointing arm of the Benito Juarez statue), then left on 23rd Street. Walk to H Street and turn right, and follow it through the campus of George Washington University, including the university yard, between 20th and 21st Streets.

Continue in the same direction on H Street. Make a left on 19th Street and a right on Pennsylvania Avenue. Just across 17th Street, you can't help but notice the multi-columned:

5. **Old Executive Office Building.** When the Iran-Contra scandal began to break in November 1986, it was as deeply disturbing as any revelation from Washington since Watergate. The Reagan administration, in its zeal to topple the socialist Sandinista government in Nicaragua, had illegally sold arms to Ayatollah Khomeini's Iran to fund a rag-tag army of "freedom fighters" in Nicaragua known as the *Contras.* There were many parallels between the two scandals: Both revealed glimpses of a secret government accountable only to the president (and that in a very hazy way), financed with ill-gotten public funds, and used to carry out policies against the express wishes of the Congress. Watergate had its "plumbers" and the "dirty-tricks" committee; Iran-Contra had CIA director William Casey speaking approvingly to Oliver North of a permanent, "off the shelf, self-sustaining, stand-alone entity that could perform certain activities on behalf of the United States." In the sanctimonious North, Iran-Contra had its very own G. Gordon Liddy. North was the chief architect of the Iran-Contra policy, which political analyst Frances Fitzgerald called "as stupid as any since the Trojans took in that gigantic wooden horse"; But during the congressional hearings into the matter in 1987, North somehow became a hero to many by virtue of his G.I.-Joe persona and such flag-waving statements as this one: "I am proud to work for that commander-in-chief. And if the commander-in-chief tells this lieutenant colonel to go stand in the corner and sit on his head, I will do so."

But history did not quite repeat itself. In the bowels of this enormous gray building, North and his pretty blond secretary, Fawn Hall, showed that the misfortunes endured by Nixon and his staff had not been in vain: Determined not to leave a smoking gun on the order of Nixon's White House tapes, they shredded evidence of the affair. Through their efforts and the stubborn resistance of Reagan and his officials to congressional questions about the imbroglio ("I can't recall" became a refrain throughout the hearings), most of the miscreants got off with a slap on the wrist or scot-free. Hall—who concisely captured the spirit of Iran-Contra when she told Congress, "Sometimes you have to go above the written law"—later tried to cash in on her involvement with the affair, signing with the William Morris talent agency. In 1994 she turned up again, on her way into a rehab center for treatment of cocaine addiction. Oliver North has made the most of his notoriety, publishing a book in 1991 and making a strong run for the U.S. senate in Virginia in 1994. Ronald Reagan's "Teflon" reputation was finally tarnished by Iran-Contra; either he lied in steadfastly denying involvement in the cloak-and-dagger theatrics of his subordinates, or he was troublingly out of touch with the policies perpetrated in his name. If it's the latter, perhaps, when he said "Every night I go to bed knowing that there are things that I am not aware of," he was justifiably paranoid.

Across Pennsylvania Avenue from the Old Executive Office Building (it's just past the Renwick Gallery), the brick house with the dormer windows is:

6. **Lee House** (built 1824), which, with the adjacent **Blair House** (built 1858), has served as the president's official guesthouse since 1943. Blair House was once the home of Montgomery Blair, the attorney of Dred Scott, a slave who wanted to be declared a free man because he had lived for a time with his master in a free territory. His case made its way to the Supreme Court in 1857, at which point it became a focal point in the struggle over slavery in the new territories between abolitionist and proslavery forces. With the nation looking to the court to solve a problem Congress could not, Chief Justice Roger B. Taney (a southerner) delivered the infamous majority opinion that a Negro had no rights that "a white man was bound to respect;" therefore, Scott's case had no merit. Abolitionists were outraged, and the nation moved within a hair's breadth of civil war.

In this house, Robert E. Lee was offered the command of the Union Army. Though he supported the Union, he was finally more loyal to his home state of Virginia. He turned the offer down, creating a furor in the federal capital.

Continuing along Pennsylvania Avenue, you'll cross Jackson Place and come to:

7. **Lafayette Square.** This small public park, its Pennsylvania Avenue side flanked by heroic statues of Rochambeau and Lafayette, has been the site of several dark incidents. In 1859 Daniel Sickles, a congressman from New York, discovered that his friend Philip Barton Key (whose father was Francis Scott Key, author of "The Star-Spangled Banner") had been carrying on an affair with his wife, Teresa. When Key next signaled Teresa from Lafayette Square outside the Sickles' window, the infuriated Sickles rushed outside and shot Key dead. The murder sparked the sort of sensational tabloid coverage commonplace today. When the case came to trial, Sickles's lawyer successfully made use of a "temporary insanity" defense, and his client was acquitted. Afterward, however, Sickles was anything but repentant: "Of course I intended to kill him," he told friends, "He deserved it."

In 1917 women's suffragists demonstrated in Lafayette Square and were arrested, charged with "obstructing traffic." Among them was Alice Paul, founder of the National Woman's Party in 1913 and author of the Equal Rights Amendment in 1923. Paul and the other women were jailed in the abandoned Occoquan Workhouse, where they had to sleep on the floor and were given food filled with worms. When they chose to go on a hunger strike, they were force-fed with tubes stuck up their nostrils and down their throats. Women's right to vote would not be ratified until 1920.

Lafayette Square continues to be a focal point for protests by citizens and groups that find the actions, or inaction, of the government scandalous in one way or another. Many consider it scandalous as well that the park is filled with homeless people, especially since it lies directly across the street from the:

8. **White House.** Many who've held the highest office in the land rose to the top precisely because they were ruthless and unprincipled, so it should come as no surprise that the White House's history is stained with scandal. John F. Kennedy was not the only president to enjoy illicit passion

within these walls. Warren G. Harding, president from 1921 until his death in 1923, was reported to have enjoyed the favors of mistress Nan Britton in a closet near the Oval Office—the family dog once sniffed them out there. (Britton, 30 years Harding's junior, had a daughter she alleged was conceived with Harding on the couch of his office when he was a senator. After his death she tried unsuccessfully to get a portion of his estate for her child and in 1927 published a bestseller called *The President's Daughter*. It was dedicated to "all unwed mothers, and to their innocent children whose fathers usually are not known to the world.") Before he was president, Harding carried on a 15-year affair with Carrie Fulton Phillips, a German sympathizer and the wife of an old friend. The Hardings and the Phillipses socialized and even took trips together. When Harding ran for the presidency, the secret service paid off the couple and continued to supply them with "hush money" until Harding's death.

Harding had much more serious trouble in his choice of friends than with women. During his short term, a long list of his close associates, most of them part of what was called the "Ohio gang," made fast money brokering shady deals in smoke-filled rooms. Though he publicly lauded Prohibition, he was an eager participant in all-night White House poker games with his cronies, at which a full compliment of illegal alcohol was available. Washington insider Alice Roosevelt Longworth, daughter of Teddy Roosevelt, considered him a "slob" who imbued his White House "with the air of a loose speakeasy." The most infamous scandal attributed to his venal associates was Teapot Dome, in which two cabinet ministers earned enormous kickbacks from private oilmen in exchange for turning over two huge government oil reserves to them for peanuts. Not long before he died, Harding said, "I can take care of my enemies all right. But my friends, my God-damn friends . . . they're the ones who keep me walking the floor nights." It's no wonder he keeled over from a heart attack.

Franklin Delano Roosevelt allegedly had lovers in the White House: lifetime love Lucy Mercer and his secretary Missy Lehand. Lucy Mercer was with FDR when he died in Warm Springs, Georgia, but she discreetly departed before Eleanor arrived.

Through the years, certain White House wives have been known for their eccentricities in personality or spending. Mary Todd Lincoln, who was often ill-tempered and mentally unstable, got so carried away while redecorating the White House that she overran by $6,700 a hefty appropriation of $20,000. When he got wind of his wife's profligate spending, Honest Abe was incensed: "[The overrun] can never have my approval," he fumed. "I'll pay it out of my own pocket first—it would stink in the nostrils of the American people to have it said the President of the United States had approved a bill overrunning an appropriation of $20,000 for *flub dubs,* for this damned old house, when the soldiers cannot have blankets!"

Jackie Kennedy, who observed upon arrival at the White House that "it looked as though furnished from discount stores," fought off rumors of her husband's womanizing with lavish spending on furnishings and her own wardrobe. Nancy Reagan, on the other hand, merely "borrowed" the designer clothes she wore.

Perhaps the most reviled of all presidential wives was Edith Bolling Wilson (a great granddaughter of Pocahontas), who, for all intents and purposes, ran the White House for a year and a half after Woodrow Wilson suffered a severe stroke in 1919. He was left partially paralyzed and was often bedridden, but the severity of his condition was kept a secret from the American people. Edith screened all his memos and callers, essentially determining matters of state. Unlike Mary Todd Lincoln and Jackie Kennedy, Edith Wilson was a frugal first lady; during World War I, she put sheep to graze on the White House lawn rather than pay someone to mow it.

Her books written from the viewpoint of Millie the family dog notwithstanding, George Bush's housewifely spouse, Barbara, was popular with the public. Chief of Staff John Sununu, the "fat little pirate" (so-called by a Bush staffer) who was Bush's right-hand man through the 1988 campaign and the early years of his presidency, was not. The bumptious, relentlessly abrasive former governor of New Hampshire ruffled feathers all over Washington. When it was revealed that he had a penchant for using government jets and limos for pleasure trips, his downfall was swift and unceremonious. He resigned in December 1991; when the news was announced a senior White House official greeted a reporter's call by singing, "Ding, dong, the witch is dead. . . . "

Next to the White House, on Pennsylvania Avenue between Madison Avenue and 15th Street, stands the:

9. **Treasury Department,** fronted by an Ionic colonnade under a pediment. The nation's first Secretary of the Treasury, the brilliant, tempestuous Alexander Hamilton, saw his presidential ambitions wrecked on the shoals of his affair with a married woman named Maria Reynolds. Reynolds's unscrupulous husband, James, didn't mind the affair at all; he began leaning on Hamilton for small sums to keep his mouth shut. Hamilton continued seeing Maria and paying off her husband for some years, until Mr. Reynolds, finding himself in hot water with the law, asked Hamilton to pull some strings for him. When Hamilton refused, Reynolds made good on his threat to publish the sordid details of the affair. Hamilton responded by publishing his own version of events. In a humiliating public confession on the level of televangelist Jimmy Swaggart's, he described his affair as "an amorous connection, detected . . . by the husband, imposing on me the necessity of a pecuniary composition with him, and leaving me afterwards under a duress for fear of disclosure . . . There is nothing worse in the affair than an irregular and indelicate amour . . . I have paid pretty severely for the folly and can never recollect it without disgust and self condemnation." As news of Hamilton's pamphlet spread, the statesman became the laughingstock of his Federalist party; all hopes of higher office were lost to him. He was killed in a duel with Aaron Burr on July 11, 1804—not over love, but politics.

Take a Break You'll pass the **Old Ebbitt Grill,** 675 15th Street NW, at G Street (tel. 202/347-4801), a landmark Washington restaurant, on your left en route to your next stop, the Willard. It has stood at two other nearby locations: One was two doors down from Rhodes Tavern, where it is said British generals toasted each other as they watched Washington burn during the War of 1812. Though its interior is ultra elegant—with bevelled mirrors, gaslight sconces, etched-glass panels, and Persian rugs strewn on beautiful oak and marble floors—prices are moderate. The menu changes daily; lunch entrées might range from burgers to pasta dishes to a fried oyster sandwich or crabcake platter. Lunch is served Monday through Friday from 11am to 5pm and Saturday from 11:30am to 4pm; Sunday brunch is 9:30am to 4pm.

At the Treasury Department, turn right onto 15th Street and follow it to Pennsylvania Avenue. Cross 15th Street. Coming up on your left is the stately:

10. **Willard Hotel** at 1455 Pennsylvania Avenue NW. The Willard has been center stage for Washington's hardball politics and seamy deals for more than 100 years. In fact, it was in the lobby of the original Willard Hotel (razed in 1901 to make way for the present structure) that the term *lobbyist* was coined. Ulysses S. Grant, who partook of many a cigar and brandy in the Willard, was often pestered here by people seeking to influence government business; hence he began to refer to them as "lobbyists." Apparently his associates peddled their influence freely—by the end of Grant's administration, his vice president, Navy Department, Department of the Interior, and Diplomatic Service were all under the cloud of scandal. During and after the Civil War, government was almost completely beholden to business; robber barons would come to places like the Willard and buy votes from politicians for a few glasses of good whisky, supplemented by satchels of cash. The wheelers and dealers got rich in the process; as labor organizer Mother Jones put it, "You steal a pair of shoes, you go to jail. You steal a railroad, and you go to the U.S. Senate."

When muckraking journalists began to publish exposés of government corruption in mass-market magazines in the first decade of the 20th century, things began to change. But the arrogance of industrialists who were used to getting their way is clear in the response banker J. P. Morgan had to a reform effort by President Theodore Roosevelt: "If we've done anything wrong," he said to the President, "send your man to see my man, and they will fix it up."

Take a minute to admire the Willard's sumptuously restored interior. Then, exit the hotel, turn right on 14th Street, and cross to the rather ornate building at the corner of 14th and Pennsylvania Avenue South, the:

11. **District Building,** headquarters of the mayor of Washington. He's baaaaaack! On January 2, 1995, "Mayor for life" Marion Barry was sworn in for a fourth term, completing one of the most improbable comebacks in American political history.

Marion Barry was busted by FBI agents after being videotaped taking two long hits from a crack pipe at the capital's Vista Hotel on January 18, 1990. The arrest ended a year's worth of ugly rumor and speculation that Barry—who presided over the nation's capital as it was consumed by an epidemic of drug use and violence, becoming the "murder capital" of the country—was himself a user. Testimony presented at Barry's trial on 11 drug charges and three perjury counts showed the mayor to be the very picture of depravity; in columnist George Hackett's words, he was "a fidgety drug addict, eager to snort cocaine or smoke crack any time, almost any place." Charles Lewis, a former city employee convicted of drug dealing in 1989, told of the numerous times he and Barry had used drugs together, the favors the mayor granted to his drug pal (with Barry's help, Lewis rose from his modest city job to broker a personnel-management deal between the District and the Virgin Islands), and of the women Barry consorted with on his frequent drugs-and-sex junkets. One of these was a former model named Rasheeda Moore, who testified at the trial that she and Barry had used drugs together "at least 100 times." It was Moore who baited the trap the FBI set for him at the Vista. A sordid, enduring image from the videotape of the arrest is the slump-shouldered, handcuffed Barry being led away, cursing Moore.

Barry surrendered his job and eventually served a six-month sentence in a federal prison in Petersburg, Virginia, where he reportedly enjoyed the attentions of a prostitute in the prison's visiting room. Thirty to 50 other inmates and guests were in the room, including one Floyd Robertson, who said "It was blatant. . . . There's no way on God's green earth anybody with . . . common sense would be able to not know what was going on in that corner." The incident surprised no one who saw Barry appear on the *Sally Jessy Raphaël* show to talk about his sexual addiction. Of his compulsive womanizing, Barry said "It was all part of the addiction. This disease is cunning, baffling, powerful. It destroys your judgment." Incredibly, the people of Washington, D.C.—despite his well-documented lapses in judgment, despite the fact that 14 members of his administration had been found guilty of fiscal wrongdoing—decided in November 1994 to return Marion Barry to his office in this building.

Continue on Pennsylvania Avenue toward the Capitol dome, walking through:

12. **Freedom Plaza.** On the upper terrace of the plaza is part of Pierre Charles L'Enfant's original plan for the federal capital, rendered in black and white stone and bookended by a fountain at one end and an equestrian statue of General Pulaski at the other. L'Enfant laid out the city with sweeping diagonal boulevards, open plazas, and circles, but his impetuous behavior and penchant for ignoring orders, overspending his budgets, and disregarding landowners with prior claims led George Washington to relieve him of his duties after only a year. One of his coworkers, Benjamin Banneker, a freed slave who worked as a surveyor, made a copy of L'Enfant's blueprints from memory, and the city the Frenchman envisioned was ultimately built—without just remuneration for its creator. L'Enfant became obsessed with making ever more fantastic claims against the government (he asked for $95,000; the federal government offered $35,000), and lived the rest of his life on the charity of friends. He died penniless in Maryland.

Proceed along Pennsylvania Avenue to 12th Street. On your right, in front of the Old Post Office, is a:

13. **statue of Benjamin Franklin,** which pays homage to this Renaissance man of America's early years. Over the course of his life he was many things—printer, writer, scientist, patriot, and diplomat—but with his wit, urbanity, and joy in the pleasures of life, he was also a notorious rake. Although he wrote an essay called "Eight Reasons Older Women Are Preferable to Younger Women" later in his life, he had an illegitimate son with a younger woman and had the nerve to ask his (older) wife to raise the child. She did, and the biological mother moved into their home and worked as a maid. Franklin never tried to hide the

affair or the child (perhaps that's why nothing much was made of it in the pages of history), and the boy, William, grew up to become governor of New Jersey.

Note: Though it's not an official refreshment stop, there are several restaurants in a food court inside the Old Post Office. Whether you stop in for a bite or not, its stunning Romanesque interior merits a look.

The building festooned with flags at Pennsylvania Avenue and 10th Street is the headquarters of the:

14. **Federal Bureau of Investigation (FBI),** which aggressively fills the block. The building takes its name from the Bureau's first director, J. Edgar Hoover. Hoover built the new agency into a law enforcement empire and became enormously powerful in the process, running his fief with scant interference through the tenures of eight presidents (1924–72). By the time he died in 1972, Hoover was feared and hated by millions for his agency's habit of bending civil liberties laws, especially when gathering information on suspected "subversives"—nonconformists of any stripe. After his death, rumors of misuse of FBI funds and other abuses of office began to percolate, but the death blow to Hoover's status as an American icon came with the publication of Anthony Summers's *Official and Confidential* (1993). The book's revelations about Hoover's homosexuality, transvestitism, and 42-year-long relationship with Clyde Tolson (Hoover's right hand at the FBI) were notable on one hand because, as columnist Frank Rich noted, "For connoisseurs of hypocrisy, it is hard to beat the spectacle of our No. 1 G-man—the puritanical, blackmailing spy on the sex lives of Martin Luther King and the Kennedys, the malicious persecutor of 'sex deviates'—getting all dolled up in . . . cunning little cocktail ensembles." But much more serious is Summers's finding that mobster Meyer Lansky and others in organized crime allegedly obtained pictures of Hoover and Tolson having sex and used them to blackmail Hoover into protecting them from major prosecutions.

Continue along Pennsylvania Avenue. On your left, between 8th and 9th Streets, is the:

15. **United States Naval Memorial,** depicting a lone sailor surveying the world's bodies of water. Around the outside

of the monument achievements in naval history are represented. The navy has found the 1990s rough going. A
22-year-old radioman named Allen Schindler was harassed
"24 hours a day" by shipmates aboard the U.S.S. *Belleau
Wood* after they found out he was gay; in October 1992,
he was beaten to death by fellow sailor Terry Helvey. There
have been several other instances of gay-bashing involving
sailors in recent years. In December 1993, three young and
promising officers stationed in Coronado, California, became entangled in an amorous triangle that ended in a
double murder and suicide. But the most far-reaching
scandal to touch the navy in many years is the deplorable
behavior of naval aviators at their 1991 Tailhook Association convention in Las Vegas. In a scene that would have
made *Animal House*'s parties look like polite wine-and-cheese
affairs, a mob of drunken fliers assaulted and sexually
molested 26 women, many of them naval officers, in the
hallways of the Las Vegas Hilton. Many senior navy officials were in the hotel at the time, and, as one outraged
victim said, "Not one of them said, 'Stop!'"

☕ Take a Break   Adjacent to the Naval Memorial is
the **Peasant Restaurant & Bar,** 801 Pennsylvania
Avenue NW (tel. 202/638-2140). Though its name
belies a plush interior—with crisply white-linened
tables amid potted palms, elegant brass chandeliers, and
mahogany-wainscoted cream walls hung with turn-of-
the-century French silhouette portraits—prices are quite
moderate for such a sumptuous setting. (Weather permitting, there are also café tables on Naval Memorial Plaza.)
So large are portions here, you could dine on appetizers
(such as plump scallion-studded crabcakes served with
fresh tomato salsa), leaving room for a sizeable wedge of
chocolate toffee pie smothered in whipped cream, hot
caramel, and chocolate-covered toffee. The Peasant is open
for lunch Monday through Friday only from 11am to 3pm;
dinner is served Monday through Saturday from 5:30pm,
Sunday 5pm.

And speaking of dining on appetizers, another great
choice in this area is **Jaleo,** a Spanish regional/tapas restaurant at 480 7th Street NW, at E Street (tel. 202/628-7949).
Housed in the Civil War–era Lansburgh Building, Jaleo is

exuberantly colorful, with a casual-chic interior focusing on a large mural of a flamenco dancer based on John Singer Sargeant's painting, *Jaleo*. Background music appropriately ranges from the Gypsy Kings to Spanish guitar. A meal here consists of a variety of small dishes—perhaps *patatas bravas* (crisp-fried chunks of red potato topped with a piquant chili sauce and aïoli), marinated steamed mussels served on a bed of haricots verts, and eggplant flan with red pepper sauce. Most dishes are under $5. Jaleo is open for lunch Monday through Saturday from 11:30am to 2:30pm, with a limited tapas menu from 2:30 to 5:30pm; dinner is served nightly from 5:30pm.

Farther east, Pennsylvania Avenue runs directly into the:

16. **Capitol.** You're looking at its west, or back, side, the only part of the facade that dates to the original building, the cornerstone of which was laid by George Washington himself. Capitol architect Benjamin Latrobe died prematurely in an accident here; he was killed when construction superintendent John Lenthall removed a support arch that Latrobe deemed necessary, causing part of the building to collapse on top of the unfortunate Latrobe.

The House of Representatives (to the right of the dome) and the Senate (to the left) have produced their share of scoundrels. The Democrats, it's said, get in trouble with sex and the Republicans with money, but there have been some crossovers.

Where to begin? Perhaps the most unsavory senator of all (and it had nothing to do with sex or money, but with fear) was Joseph P. McCarthy (R-Wisconsin, 1947–57), who conducted a heavy-handed witch hunt of Communists and alleged Communists, resorting to "guilt-by-association" and scare tactics.

When it comes to drinking and womanizing, the person who most readily comes to mind is Massachusetts senator Ted Kennedy, whose life could be characterized as one long scandal—from Chappaquiddick and the tragic drowning of Mary Jo Kopeckne to the Palm Beach "incident" in which his nephew William Kennedy Smith was accused (and acquitted) of raping a woman at the family vacation compound on Easter weekend in 1991 (Ted Kennedy was at the estate at the time).

Gary Hart, Democratic senator from Colorado, was within reach of his party's presidential nomination in 1987 when he was caught by two pesky reporters from the *Miami Herald* leaving through the back door of his Capitol Hill townhouse with shapely Donna Rice. A furor ensued over the former divinity professor's ethics; when reports uncovered evidence of yet more adulterous liaisons, he was forced to abandon his presidential ambitions for the dubious consolation of becoming the butt of David Letterman's jokes. ("Top Ten List of Gary Hart Pick-Up Lines: 'Can a Kennedyesque guy buy you a drink?' 'Have you ever seen a frontrunner naked?'" etc.)

On October 7, 1974, Wilbur Mills, Arkansas congressman and Chairman of the House Ways and Means Committee, was stopped by police at Washington's cherry-tree-lined Tidal Basin at 2am for speeding and driving without headlights on. His date for the evening, professional stripper Fanne Foxe, also known as the "Argentine firecracker," panicked and plunged into the Basin, taking Mills' career straight into the drink with her.

South Carolina Congressman John Jenrette was already under investigation for selling underwater land in Florida when his name was linked to Abscam. He and a few of his associates were caught selling Congressional favors to men they thought were Arab sheiks but were really FBI agents. In the tape that was made of a deal in action, Jenrette admitted, "I've got larceny in my heart." The equally pleasant crook and congressman Michael Meyer simply said, "Bullshit walks, money talks." To top off the whole mess, Jenrette and his wife Rita were spotted having sex one night on the steps of the Capitol's west side. Jenrette was later arrested for shoplifting shoes and ties, and the now ex–Mrs. Jenrette wrote a tell-all tome called *My Capitol Secrets,* then exposed herself even more fully to the public in *Playboy* magazine.

Barney Frank, Democratic congressman from Massachusetts, made the headlines in 1990 when it was disclosed that his boyfriend was running a male prostitution ring out of Frank's Capitol Hill townhouse.

And in fall 1991, taxpayers were horrified to learn that 252 members of the House of Representatives and 51 former members had overdrafts (many into the thousands of dollars) with the House Bank.

Walk around the Capitol and make your way to the imposing:

17. **Supreme Court.** In 1963 and 1964, the Warren Commission, led by Chief Justice Earl Warren (who served from 1953 to 1969), investigated the assassination of John F. Kennedy and determined that gunman Lee Harvey Oswald acted alone, a decision that few believe today. This could be the major cover-up of the century.

On October 15, 1991, Clarence Thomas, who had been chairman of the Equal Employment Opportunity Commission under President Ronald Reagan, became the 106th Supreme Court justice, but not without great controversy. At his confirmation hearing, a former aide, Anita Hill, leveled charges of sexual harassment against Thomas, who labeled it "high-tech lynching." Thomas and Hill came to the hearings with sparkling reputations for character and integrity: Hill calmly delivered her specific, graphic testimony, and Thomas responded with agonized denials. In the end, the only clarities revealed were that either Hill or Thomas was a monumental liar, and that these two people had been swept up by the relentless undertows of partisan politics and the media's scandal machine. Thomas was confirmed by the Senate by a two-vote margin.

Some say Hill's action made it easier for other women to come forward in sexual-abuse situations. Case in point: In November 1992, 10 women pressed charges of sexual harassment against Oregon senator Bob Packwood, who managed to keep the allegations quiet until after his reelection.

Stay tuned for upcoming scandals.

From here, you can get the Metro at either Judiciary Square, Federal Center SW, or Union Station.

EMBASSY ROW

Start: Dupont Circle.

Metro: Dupont Circle, south exit.

Finish: Washington Cathedral.

Time: Approximately 3½ hours.

Best Times: Any day is good. If you want to explore the National Cathedral, plan to wind up there in time for a tour (see Stop 34 below).

Note: Women should bring a scarf or hat; a head covering is required for them at the Islamic Center mosque. Shorts and short skirts are also forbidden.

Massachusetts Avenue, Washington's longest thoroughfare, runs parallel to Pennsylvania Avenue but extends north of it past American University and goes on into Maryland. The stretch between Dupont Circle and Observatory Circle is known as Embassy Row because it has the greatest concentration of the city's embassies and chanceries. Most were built as luxurious private houses between 1890 and 1930 and are stunning in their beaux-arts splendor. The first embassies to move into the neighborhood, starting a popular trend, were those of Great Britain and Brazil. Massachusetts Avenue addresses are now so popular that if one embassy vacates a house, another will immediately move in.

This tour encompasses the Massachusetts Avenue embassies as well as other attractions close by and en route. Though most embassies are not open to the public, their exterior architecture alone makes for an aesthetically thrilling walk.

• • • • • • • • • • • • • • • •

Begin where you exited the Metro, at the south side of tree-filled:

1. **Dupont Circle.** The hub of Washington's most patrician turn-of-the-century neighborhood, Dupont Circle today is peopled by everyday folk—sunbathers, musicians, chess players, occasional political demonstrators, and young lovers, both straight and gay. But many of the magnificent mansions that lined the streets radiating from it still exist, evoking the vainglorious excesses of the Gilded Age. The park itself honors Admiral Samuel Francis du Pont (1803–65)—a Civil War hero who served in the U.S. Navy—for distinguished services to his country. Subjecting his fleet of 17 ships to a massive exchange of cannon fire, he captured a pair of Confederate forts along Port Royal Sound in South Carolina, securing the area as an important Union navy base. Originally, a small bronze equestrian statue of du Pont was erected in the center of the circle, but his status-conscious family, feeling something more upscale was in order, hired no less than Lincoln Memorial–designers Daniel Chester French and Henry Bacon to create something more grandiose. The figures at the base of the fountain represent the stars, the sea, and the wind—all essential elements for a sailor.

The impressive building to your right at P Street and Dupont Circle is the neoclassical Italianate:

2. **Patterson House,** 15 Dupont Circle NW, designed by architect Stanford White. Built at the turn of the century, this was for many years the backdrop for glamorous social gatherings in the city. President and Mrs. Calvin Coolidge were houseguests here while the White House was undergoing renovation in 1927, and Charles Lindbergh was the guest of honor when he returned from the transatlantic flight that made him a hero to the nation. Lindbergh stood at the

second-story balcony and greeted the enthusiastic well-wishers gathered in Dupont Circle. When the house's owner, Cissy Patterson, a socialite and the owner of *The Washington Times-Herald,* died in 1948, the house was donated to the Red Cross, which in turn sold it in 1951 to the Washington Club, an exclusive private women's club. Asked what the club does, one member replied, "Basically, we have ambassadors to dinner." Free 20-minute guided tours are given Monday, Wednesday, and Friday between 9:30 and 11:30am. Call 202/483-9200 for details.

Take a Break **Kramerbooks & Afterwords, A Café,** just off Dupont Circle at 1517 Connecticut Street NW (tel. 202/387-1462), was a bookstore-cum-café long before the current craze for such combinations. It offers seating in a cozy room under a low beamed ceiling, in a sun-drenched solarium, and outdoors at café tables. You can stop here for a pre-tour breakfast (it opens at 7:30am daily). The rest of the day an eclectic menu offers nachos, salads, sandwiches, and pasta dishes. There's a full bar.

Pick up Massachusetts Avenue directly across Dupont Circle from Patterson House. As you proceed, the even-numbered buildings will be on your left, the odd-numbered on your right. At no. 2000 is:

3. **Blaine Mansion** (1881), a striking red-brick building, with green decorative motifs on the carriage porch in the style of paper cutouts. This eclectic architectural wonder (the *AIA Guide to the Architecture of Washington, D.C.* calls it "brooding and grim" and a "craggy pile" that "glowers at passersby as if to express disapproval of the neighborhood's present commercial bustle") was originally the home of James Gillespie Blaine (1830–93). A post–Civil War Republican and reconstructionist, he served as a congressman, senator, Speaker of the House, and secretary of state (under James Garfield and William Henry Harrison). Between 1876 and 1892, he made four unsuccessful bids for the presidency. Blaine's career was marked by allegations of corruption; political opponents dubbed him "Slippery Jim." Corruption or no, he eventually found upkeep of this vast residence too costly. Inventor George Westinghouse (a pioneer in the use of high-voltage AC electricity, creator of

an air brake for railways, and founder of the Westinghouse Electric Company) bought it in 1901 and lived here until his death in 1914. The mansion has been used as commercial space since the late 1940s.

Nearby is:

4. **2012 Massachusetts Avenue,** since 1957 the national headquarters for the Business & Professional Women's Clubs and the Business & Professional Women's Foundation, which work together to promote full participation/equality in the workplace and economic self-sufficiency for working women through education, information, and research. The five-story Georgian/Italian-Renaissance Revival brick-and-sandstone edifice was designed by Glenn Brown for the Joseph Beale family in 1898. In 1904, it was purchased by Samuel Spencer, a one-time partner of J. P. Morgan and Company and the first president of the Southern Railroad. Feel free to walk in and admire the sitting room to the left of the entry, the rich oak paneling, the fluted Ionic oak columns in the lobby, and the gorgeous staircase with its intricately tooled banister. You may also visit the Marguerite Rawalt Resource Center, a library housing comprehensive information on working women's issues, at the rear of the first floor. The building was renovated in 1988. Note the commemorative bricks out front honoring various members.

On the corner, at no. 2020, is the 60-room:

5. **Walsh Mansion (Indonesian embassy),** happily open to the public. This is an edifice of awe-inspiring splendor, with a three-story-high entrance hall, a mansard roof, an art nouveau carved-mahogany grand staircase, a magnificent stained-glass skylight illuminating the central hall, and gorgeous gilded floral-motif torchiers. Its plush interior is today enhanced by an overlay of Indonesian opulence, which, interestingly enough, harmonizes very well with the mansion's intrinsic aesthetic. Ionic marble columns at the entrance are flanked by fierce-looking statues from Bali (said to ward off evil and attract good). The Garuda Room, which centers on a massive baroque-style wood organ, houses richly carved display cases filled with art, beadwork, silver, carvings, and curios from various provinces of Indonesia. And

the Gamelan Room—today used for *gamelan* concerts and *wayang* (shadow puppetry)—occupies a Louis XIV–style salon with rose damask wall coverings and an ornate ceiling that is embellished with angels and elaborately bordered by gilt-trimmed swags, shells, and sprays. The gamelan—an Indonesian orchestra comprised of a set of instruments whose music is said to be like "moonlight and flowing water"—was an inspiration to Debussy.

The beaux-arts mansion, today on the National Register of Historic Places, was built in 1903 for Thomas Walsh, an Irishman from Tipperary who struck it rich (to the tune of $43 million!) in the gold mines of Colorado. Henry Andersen, a Danish immigrant, was the architect. Walsh embedded a slab of gold ore in the front porch, symbolizing the source of his wealth. The family entertained lavishly; guests included Admiral George Dewey, President Theodore Roosevelt's daughter Alice (the Walshes gave a ball and cotillion in her honor), senators, cabinet members, foreign ministers, and visiting royalty (including King Leopold III of Belgium, among others). Ostentatious formal dinners were eaten with flatware fashioned from glittering nuggets mined by Walsh.

Money and a fine house, however, didn't ensure Walsh's happiness; he died a recluse in 1910. Walsh's daughter Evalyn inherited the mansion. In 1908, she married newspaper magnate Edward McLean, whose family owned the *Washington Post;* they lived here from 1912 to 1916. During World War II, the mansion was used, rent free, by the Washington chapter of the the American Red Cross. Evalyn sold it to the government of Indonesia for $335,000 in 1951—a pittance in today's real estate market and even then only a tenth of the mansion's original cost. Probably she needed the money. The McLean's had lived it up in Gilded Age style; one Christmas it was reported they spent $40,000 in gifts for their young son! They squandered the vast fortunes—amounting to over $100 million—of both of their families. Evalyn was the last private owner of the Hope Diamond, the largest blue diamond in existence; it is now displayed in the National Museum of Natural History.

Where Massachusetts Avenue, 21st Street, and Q Street meet is the impressive:

Embassy Row

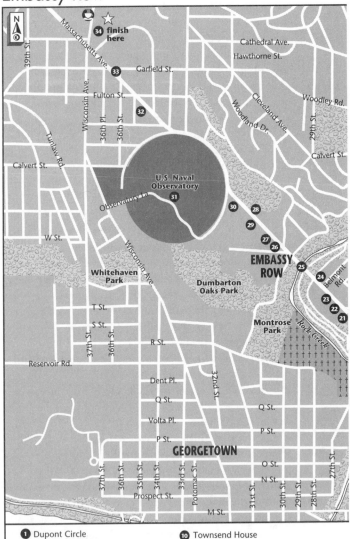

1. Dupont Circle
2. Patterson House
3. Blaine Mansion
4. 2012 Massachusetts Avenue
5. Walsh Mansion
   (Indonesian Embassy)
6. Phillips Collection of
   Modern Art
7. Moroccan Embassy
8. Indian Embassy
9. Anderson House
10. Townsend House
11. Presbyterian Church of the Pilgrims
12. Residence of the Ambassador of
    Luxembourg
13. Headquarters of the National Society
    Daughters of the American Colonists
14. Jennings House
15. Irish Embassy
16. Residence of the Turkish Ambassador
17. Sheridan Circle
18. Barney Studio House

9652

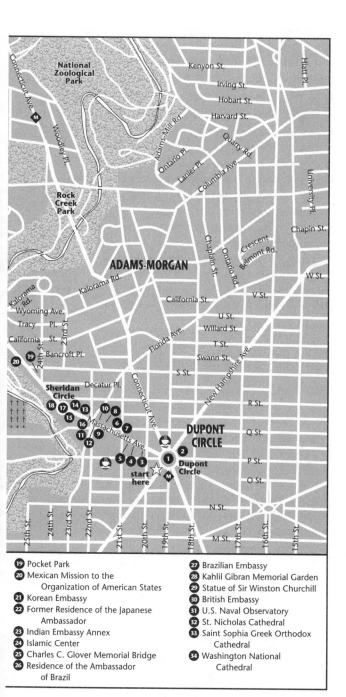

19 Pocket Park
20 Mexican Mission to the
        Organization of American States
21 Korean Embassy
22 Former Residence of the Japanese
        Ambassador
23 Indian Embassy Annex
24 Islamic Center
25 Charles C. Glover Memorial Bridge
26 Residence of the Ambassador
        of Brazil
27 Brazilian Embassy
28 Kahlil Gibran Memorial Garden
29 Statue of Sir Winston Churchill
30 British Embassy
31 U.S. Naval Observatory
32 St. Nicholas Cathedral
33 Saint Sophia Greek Orthodox
        Cathedral
34 Washington National
        Cathedral

The Curse of the Hope Diamond

Evalyn Walsh first spotted the sapphire-blue 45.5-carat Hope Diamond adorning the neck of a sultan's harem girl in Turkey. Though she scoffed at stories of "the curse," Evalyn had a priest bless the stone after she purchased it. According to legend, the diamond was originally the eye of an ancient Indian idol. It was stolen from India by a French adventurer, who smuggled the gem into Paris—shortly before he was torn apart by wild dogs! The doomed diamond eventually turned up in the court of Louis XIV, ostensibly precipitating the deaths of the monarch's eldest son, a grandson, and a great-grandson. The stone stayed in French royal hands through the reign of Louis XVI and Marie Antoinette, who were, of course, beheaded. The diamond next appeared in Amsterdam in the hands of a jeweler, whose son stole it; later remorseful, he committed suicide.

In 1830, it was acquired by British banker Henry Thomas Hope, whose name has remained associated with it. Hope himself escaped the curse, but his grandson and heir died a pauper. The next owner was Catherine the Great of Russia; the diamond, no doubt, was the unseen force behind all those love affairs and court intrigues. And that brings us to the Turkish sultan—the gem merchant who delivered the stone to him died soon after in a car accident, along with his wife and children. And what of Evalyn Walsh McLean? Her son was killed by a car, her daughter committed suicide, and her husband, Edward McLean, was implicated in the Teapot Dome scandal and took to drink. Their marriage hit the rocks, and McLean was deemed insane and confined to a mental institution.

When Evalyn Walsh died in 1947, the Hope went to diamond merchant Harry Winston, who offered it on permanent loan to the Smithsonian Institution. The parcel proved tragic to the carrier who delivered it. His legs were crushed when he was run over by a truck, his wife died of a heart attack, his dog hung himself in a freak accident, and his house burned down. At this writing, however, the Smithsonian still seems to be in pretty good shape.

6. **Phillips Collection of Modern Art,** described in detail in the "Dupont Circle Museums" tour (Walking Tour 4). On the ground floor is a charming little café, as well as restrooms and a telephone.

   Opposite the Phillips Collection, at 1601 21st Street, is the:

7. **Moroccan embassy,** a turn-of-the-century white brick building with a tower. The Phillips Collection's next-door neighbor on Massachusetts Avenue is the:

8. **Indian embassy,** at no. 2107. On the ground floor you'll find a pleasant, sun-filled reading room packed with books, magazines, and newspapers. The elegant lobby (note its intricately carved moldings) is used for changing art exhibits. Photographs of Indian leaders also grace the walls. It's open to the public Monday through Friday from 9:30am to 6pm.

   Across the street, at no. 2118, is the 50-room:

9. **Anderson House,** home to the patriotic Society of the Cincinnati, founded in 1783. The house was built between 1903 and 1905 by Larz Anderson, a diplomat, world traveler, and a society founder. See the "Dupont Circle Museums" tour (Walking Tour 4) for more information.

   Across the street, at no. 2121, is the:

10. **Townsend House,** a magnificent limestone-walled "château" designed by the very prestigious firm of Carrère and Hastings (they were the architects of, among other things, New York's Public Library). Its inspiration was the Petit Trianon at Versailles. Frederick Law Olmsted did the landscaping. The central part of the French Renaissance house was built in 1873. In 1898, it was acquired by Mary Scott Townsend, heiress to the Pennsylvania Railroad fortune, and her husband, Richard Townsend, president of the Erie and Pittsburgh Railroad. For a rather odd reason, they built their new house around the older one; a gypsy had once warned Mrs. Townsend that she was destined to die "under a new roof." She didn't die, but Richard did, tragically, in a riding accident in 1902. Mary continued to live here until her death in 1931, entertaining, with the help of several dozen servants, on a grand scale. The Townsend's daughter, Mathilde, married Sumner Welles, who served as

Under Secretary of State for Franklin Delano Roosevelt. The Roosevelts were house guests here for several weeks before moving into the White House. Unfortunately, you can't really go in and explore the palatial interior rooms, but you can peek inside at the marble columns, the beautiful wrought-iron railing of the sinuous stairway, the marble floor, and the striking fireplaces. You may also get a glimpse of the adjoining private garden.

The house became headquarters of the exclusive Cosmos Club in 1950. Members of this private club, described as "individuals of distinction, character, and sociability," have included three presidents, 29 Nobel Prize winners, and 50 Pulitzer Prize winners. The club was founded in 1878 by men active in science, literature, and the arts; only since June 1988, have women been eligible for membership. Members have included Sinclair Lewis, Henry Kissinger, William Allen White, Herman Wouk, Archibald MacLeish, Allen Drury, Wilbur and Orville Wright, Walter Lippmann, George Bundy, and Helen Hayes.

At Massachusetts Avenue and 22nd Street, off to the left, you'll see the spire of the:

11. **Presbyterian Church of the Pilgrims.** The original church, which was on P Street, dates from 1904; this building was erected in 1929. The gas station that is cater-corner to it was built in a similar style to maintain a certain architectural tone in the neighborhood. On the lawn across the street from the church, note the statue of Taras Shevchenko (1814–61), Bard of the Ukraine. Born a serf, Shevchenko gained his freedom and went on to become a professor in Kiev. Later, his efforts towards radical social reforms led to exile in Siberia for 10 years.

Take a Break A teensy detour will take you to **Gabriel,** the handsome showplace restaurant of the Radisson-Barceló Hotel, at 2121 P Street NW (tel. 202/293-3100). This is one of my favorite D.C. restaurants—a warmly inviting and rather elegant setting for the culinary specialties of Spain and Mexico. The lunch menu runs the gamut from sandwiches (such as lamb, goat cheese, tomato, and spinach on black olive bread) to full meals like sautéed jumbo lump crabcakes with roasted corn and black-bean relish. Tapas (small tasting portions) might include fried potatoes with aïoli, dried black figs stuffed with chorizo, and crispy fried mozzarella with curried spinach. Prices are high moderate. You can have lunch here Monday through Saturday from 11:30am to 2:30pm, Sunday brunch from noon to 3pm.

In the 2200 block along Massachusetts Avenue, you'll see no. 2200, the:

12. **residence of the ambassador of Luxembourg,** a limestone Louis XV–style building fronted by a rock garden. It was begun in 1908 and completed the following year for owners Alexander and Margaret Stewart, who lived there with their three daughters. Alexander Stewart immigrated from New Brunswick, Canada, made a fortune in lumber, and served three terms as a U.S. congressman from Wisconsin. The Grand Duchess of Luxembourg, H. R. H. Charlotte, in exile during the German occupation of her country during World War II, bought the house for only $40,000 (a steal since the property even then had been assessed at $104,000); it housed the Luxembourg Legation (residence and chancery) from 1942 to 1955, and the Luxembourg embassy from 1956 to 1961. It has been the residence of the Luxembourg ambassador since 1962.

Walk past no. 2202, the **Turkish embassy's Office of the Military Attaché** (the Turkish embassy is at no. 1714 Massachusetts Avenue, on the other side of Dupont Circle); no. 2208, the **Togo embassy;** and no. 2210, the **Sudan embassy.** At no. 2205 is the:

13. **headquarters of the National Society Daughters of the American Colonists,** a four-story red brick building with bow and dormer windows and a fanlight over the door.

You'll then pass no. 2209, a beautiful building that houses the **United Arab Emirates Military Attaché Office**, and no. 2211, the **Greek Consular Office.** On the corner, at no. 2221, is the impressive:

14. **Jennings House** (1906), since 1935 the Greek embassy. The Classical Revival building and its landscaped yard originally belonged to Hennen and Mary Jennings. He was an

engineer and consultant to gold mining companies in South Africa and Venezuela, and she was a philanthropist, honored by France for her work with the American branch of the Fatherless Children of France. The couple would have been jetsetters had there been jets in their day; as it was, they enjoyed high society in London and New York. In her later years, the widowed Mary Jennings rented the house to the Greek government, and then sold it for $100,000 to a wealthy Greek-American businessman, who donated it to his mother country.

At no. 2234 is the:

15. **Irish embassy,** a lovely limestone Louis XVI–style building.

Around the corner from it, at 1607 23rd Street, is the **Romanian embassy**, which faces the stately:

16. **residence of the Turkish ambassador,** built as a private home for oilman-industrialist Edward H. Everett, who added to an already vast fortune by inventing the fluted soft-drink bottle cap. Noted architect George Oakley Totten, Jr., appropriately fronted the mansion's curved portico with fluted columns; they're crowned with rather unusual capitals that combine Ionic and Corinthian elements. If you're lucky enough to get a peek inside the stunning entry, you'll see the impressive larger-than-life bust of Mustafa Kemal, or Ataturk, founder of the republic of Turkey in 1923 and its first president. Other interior elements you won't see include a lavish Italianate ballroom, a French drawing room, an English dining room, and an indoor swimming pool—all so plush that Everett's palatial digs were nicknamed "San Simeon on the Potomac."

You've now arrived at the embassy-ringed:

17. **Sheridan Circle,** named for Civil War hero Gen. Philip Sheridan (1831–88). Honored here by an equestrian statue, Sheridan—who never lost a battle throughout his military career—was instrumental in the final encounters that led to Confederate Gen. Robert E. Lee's surrender at Appomattox in 1865. Sheridan, who also led savage attacks during Indian wars, is additionally remembered for his very un-PC statement "The only good Indian is a dead Indian." The statue is the creation of Guzon Borglum of Mount

Rushmore fame. A tragedy occurred at Sheridan Circle in 1976, when the former Chilean ambassador to the United States, Orlando Letelier, was blown up by a bomb that had been planted in his car. The incident is commemorated by a marker in front of the Romanian embassy.

At no. 2306 is the:

18. **Barney Studio House** (1902), a famous artists' salon during the lifetime of its owner, Alice Pike Barney, who was Washington's answer to Gertrude Stein. The daughter of an Ohio millionaire who married a guy like dad (another Ohio millionaire), she was a prominent member of Washington society, a painter who studied with Whistler in Paris and had a one-woman show at the Corcoran, a composer (she once scored a ballet for Russian dancer Anna Pavlova), and a writer and producer of plays. The neo-Mediterranean stucco house was designed by noted architect Waddy Wood. According to *Washington Society* magazine, Studio House was the "meeting place for wit and wisdom, genius and talent, which fine material is leavened by fashionable folk, who would like to be a bit Bohemian if they only knew how." The house, along with family furnishings and memorabilia, was donated to the Smithsonian by Barney's daughters, but it is not open to the public at this writing.

Beside the Barney Studio House at no. 2320, is the **Embassy of the Republic of Korea.** On the other side of the circle, you'll find no. 2301, the **residence of the Egyptian ambassador;** no. 2305, the residence of the Chilean ambassador; no. 2253, the **Philippine embassy;** and no. 2249, the **Kenyan embassy,** its gorgeous building sadly defaced by a hideous arcade.

Now continue along Massachusetts Avenue. Just north of the circle, on your right, are no. 2311, the stunning beaux-arts **Haitian embassy,** with its mansard roof and carved Corinthian pilasters; no 2315, the opulent **Pakistani embassy,** like the above-mentioned residence of the Turkish ambassador designed by George Oakley Totten, Jr. (note its domed tower); no. 2343, the **Croatian embassy** (fronted by a statue of St. Jerome contemplating a book); no. 2349, the **Cameroon embassy,** another George Oakley Totten, Jr., château-like mansion, this one adorned with Gothic tracery; no. 2370, a red brick building that houses the

Korean Information Center; and, next door to it, at no. 2374, the **Madagascar embassy.**

When you cross 24th Street, you'll see a:

19. **pocket park** with a statue of Irish patriot Robert Emmet (1778–1803), erected on this spot on April 22, 1966, the 50th anniversary of Irish independence. Emmet, who tried to enlist the sympathies of Napoleon and Tallyrand in the Irish cause, was the leader of an ill-conceived 1803 uprising against the British. He was captured and hanged for treason. There's a bench in the park, should you wish to rest.

To the right of the park, at no. 2401 stands the **Malaysian embassy,** opened by the prime minister of Malaysia on October 14, 1969. Across the street, at no. 2406, is the **embassy of the United Arab Emirates Residence.** Nos. 2412 and 2424 are the **Ivory Coast's consulate and embassy.**

At no. 2440 stands the:

20. **Mexican Mission to the Organization of American States,** in a modern building with stylized columns beside the windows. For many years, this was the home of architect Charles Mason Remey (1875–1975); Remey was also the first regent of the Orthodox Ba ha'i Faith, as a plaque inside the courtyard attests.

Across the street, at no. 2419, is the **Zambian embassy,** and next door at no. 2433 stands the **embassy of the Republic of the Marshall Islands.** Next to it, at no. 2443, stands the large, modern **residence** (more like a compound) **of the ambassador of Venezuela,** enclosed by a black wrought-iron fence.

At no. 2450 is the:

21. **Korean embassy,** unusual along Embassy Row because it looks more like a large office complex than the string of mansions the strip is known for. The Koreans moved in in 1992; prior to that, the building was home to the Canadian embassy, now in an ultramodern building on Pennsylvania Avenue.

At no. 2520 is the:

22. **former residence of the Japanese ambassador,** now used for social gatherings hosted by the Japanese

government. Set back from the street, with a white fence in front, it resembles a European country house—it's not a bit Asian.

Across the street, in a small brick house at no. 2511, is the embassy of the small African nation of Lesotho. No. 2536 is the:

23. **Indian embassy annex (marked by elephants at the entry),** which houses India's consular section and visa office. No. 2523 is the **Turkish embassy annex.** At no. 2535, you'll see the tidy **Belize embassy** and beyond it the minaret of the:

24. **Islamic Center,** 2551 Massachusetts Avenue. Opened in 1957, it serves as a cultural center, a place of worship for Muslims, and a facility for promoting greater understanding of their religion in America. The public is welcome to enter the mosque, which is open daily from 10am to 6pm. However, no shorts or short skirts are allowed, you have to leave your shoes on a shelf outside, and women must cover their heads. It's well worth removing your shoes to see the dazzling interior, with its intricate tilework (a gift from Turkey), marble columns, and Persian rugs (a gift from Iran). A stunning—and quite massive—brass chandelier (a gift from Egypt) is suspended from a rotunda that is embellished with 24 lovely stained-glass windows. Verses from the Koran are inscribed in mosaics above the arches in front of the pink marble–fountained courtyard, inside the colonnade, and around the 160-foot minaret from which the *Mu'azzin* announces prayer times. The building itself is tilted at an angle in order to face Mecca, its direction indicated by the *mihrab* (a small arched alcove located in the center of the front wall). To the right of the mihrab is the ebony-and ivory-inlaid *minbar* (pulpit) with over 10,000 sections forming its interlacing geometric designs.

Cross the street—the four-story brick house across from the Islamic Center, no. 2558, is the Economic & Commercial Office of the Spanish embassy—and walk across the:

25. **Charles C. Glover Memorial Bridge.** Beneath you is the Rock Creek and Potomac Parkway and the recreational path that threads through Rock Creek Park (see Walking Tour 9, "The National Zoo and Rock Creek Park").

On the other side of the bridge, on your left, the striking, three-story house with the imposing hedge at no. 3000 is the:

26. **residence of the ambassador of Brazil,** formerly the McCormick Villa (1908), fashioned along the lines of a 15th-century Roman palace. Its well-known architect, John Russell Pope, studied in Rome and is best known for the National Gallery of Art (west wing), the Jefferson Memorial, and the National Archives in Washington. Set at an angle to the lot, the house has a great deal of privacy, augmented by a sheltering hedge. Its facade features a recessed portico with four Tuscan columns modeled after a Roman palazzo. Inside (which you won't be able to see, unfortunately) is a solid silver chandelier and a curving white Italian marble stair with a bronze–and–cast-iron balustrade. The Empire-style bronze sconces on the dining room walls are said to have belonged to Josephine de Beauharnais (1763–1814), first wife of Napoleon I. The house was acquired by the Brazilian government in 1934 for $200,000.

At no. 3006, in dramatic contrast, stands the modern:

27. **Brazilian embassy,** a glass box atop a concrete slab and columns. Designed by Brazilian architect Olavo Redig de Campos, it has been called "an outstanding example of the best of contemporary architecture" by the Washington Metropolitan Chapter of the American Institute of Architects. Personally, I beg to disagree. It was built in 1971 beside an existing chancery (1935), which was then demolished and replaced by gardens. The embassy, the ambassador's home, and the nearby consulate house the embassy's large art collection, which features classics of Brazilian 20th-century painting (unfortunately, not on public view).

Across the street from the Brazilian embassy, at no. 3005, the cloistered building with the decoratively screened windows and turquoise dome is the **former Iranian embassy.** Next to it is the **South African embassy,** no. 3051, constructed here in 1965 on the site where the old Dutch-style embassy stood; beside it is the striking **ambassador's residence,** no. 3101. Most of the materials for the exterior and interior of both buildings came from South Africa. The dining room is paneled with stinkwood, which is similar to mahogany (it does not stink, despite its name).

On the other side of the street, at no. 3012, is the modern **residence of the Bolivian ambassador,** and through the adjoining gate, the **Bolivian embassy.**

Adjacent to the South African embassy is the peaceful:

28. **Kahlil Gibran Memorial Garden,** with a small bridge leading to it. The two-acre garden—a gift to the city from the Kahlil Gibran Centennial Foundation in 1991—is filled with ferns, flowers, and hedges and contains a circular wall with a bust of Gibran by Gordon S. Kray. Around it are stone benches inscribed with the words of the poet and philosopher who was born near the cedars of Lebanon and died in New York City (1883–1931). Among the quotes is one that's perfect for this spot: "We live only to discover beauty. All else is a form of waiting."

Across the street (backtracking a little) is a:

29. **statue of Sir Winston Churchill,** with one hand holding his signature cigar, the other flashing the victory sign. This work of William McVey, of Cleveland, Ohio, straddles the boundary line between the property of the British embassy and the District of Columbia to symbolize Churchill's Anglo-American parentage and his honorary citizenship in the United States. The statue was unveiled by Secretary of State Dean Rusk in 1966, on the third anniversary of Churchill's being granted U.S. citizenship.

Continue to the:

30. **British embassy,** at no. 3100, the largest British embassy in the world. It looks much like a modern-day school, except for the telltale red telephone booth at the entry. Queen Elizabeth II laid the foundation stone in 1957, and the marble slabs in the foyer list the British ambassadors to the United States from 1791 onward. The home of the ambassador, also on the property (you'll come to it first), was built in 1928 in the style of an English country house, and the red bricks of the facade were hand made in Pennsylvania to resemble those used in Tudor times in Britain. However, its architect, Sir Edwin Lutyens, in tribute to America—or perhaps to poke fun at American architectural reverence for European neoclassicism—created a colonial American facade for the building.

Around the corner from the British embassy, at Observatory Circle, is the **New Zealand embassy.** Across the street within fenced-in grounds is:

31. **U.S. Naval Observatory,** established in 1830 but called the Depot of Charts and Instruments until 1844. It was moved to this site from Foggy Bottom in 1893. The verdant grounds and lush foliage across the street make for lovely scenery as you walk. You won't be allowed to visit, but you can still see the observatory dome from the sidewalk. If you're in Washington on a Monday, try to get back to the Observatory for the 8:30 to 10pm tour of the heavens, courtesy of its astronomers and telescopes. This is a popular event; if you don't get on line by 7:30pm, you probably won't get in, especially on a clear night. They only take 90 visitors, and there's tight security. For this activity, go to the southern entrance and follow the road that runs between the British embassy and the Observatory grounds. You'll see the line. There is no planetarium at the Observatory.

The **Vice President's residence,** now the home of Al and Tipper Gore and their children, may be seen from the northern entrance, just beyond the guard station. It's the white house flying the American flag. You can usually get a brochure about the Naval Observatory from the guards, who, for security reasons, won't admit to you that it's the Vice President's residence you see.

As you walk by Observatory Circle, the steeple of the **National Cathedral** will come into view to your right. It's the last stop on this tour, and you're almost there. En route, you'll pass the site of the new **Finnish embassy,** at no. 3301. Its postmodern metal-and-glass-box architecture definitely merits a closer look. A gray-green polished-granite facade is fronted by a distressed-looking patinaed bronze lattice that is bare at this writing, but, according to plan, will soon be entwined with vines of climbing white roses, blue clematis, and ivy. Ask to be let in (people usually are) to descend the sweeping curved staircase. It leads to a dramatic window-walled central atrium (Finnish architects Mikko Heikkinen and Markku Komonen call it a "Grand Canyon") overlooking verdant woodlands, with a gangplank-like walkway under a canopy of canvas sails (reflective of

Finnish seafaring traditions), expanses of maple paneling, skylights, and minimalist copper-plated cubes.

The **Norwegian embassy** stands at 3401 Massachusetts Avenue. At no. 3415 is the **embassy of the Republic of Cape Verde**—which, if you've never heard of it, is a democratic republic in North Africa 445 miles west of Senegal. Comprised of a group of 10 volcanic islands in the Atlantic Ocean, it achieved independence in 1975, after centuries as a Portuguese colony. Some 350,000 Cape Verdean immigrants and descendants (close to the same number who populate the islands themselves) live in the United States, many of them seamen who settled in the whaling ports and mill towns of New England.

Opposite it is:

32. **St. Nicholas Cathedral,** a Russian Orthodox church, built in 1930. The church, which offers services in both English and Slavonic, is also a National War Memorial Shrine dedicated to the veterans of World War II, the Korean War, and Vietnam. Its bell tower was dedicated on December 4, 1988, the anniversary of the 1,000-year jubilee of the Russian Orthodox church.

On the opposite side of the street, at 36th Street, is another house of worship, the:

33. **Saint Sophia Greek Orthodox Cathedral.** The cornerstone was laid by President Dwight Eisenhower in 1956. In front of it is a small park, named for bishop Aimilianos Laloussis. Benches here provide a good rest stop for walkers weary of the uphill climb.

Continue to Wisconsin Avenue and turn right. You'll pass St. Albans Episcopal Church, consisting of several charming stone buildings, en route to the:

34. **Washington National Cathedral.** Dramatically positioned atop 57 acres at the city's highest point, this grand cathedral, the sixth-largest in the world, was part of Pierre L'Enfant's 18th-century plan for the capital city. It was more than a century later, however, that the foundation for his "great church for national purposes" was laid. Officially the Episcopal Cathedral Church of St. Peter and St. Paul, it is more commonly known as the National Cathedral and serves all denominations. It has been the setting for every

kind of religious service, including non-Christian ones. The foundation stone—from a field in Bethlehem, set into a piece of American granite—was laid in 1907 using the mallet with which George Washington set the cornerstone of the Capitol. Almost a century in construction, it was finally completed in 1990 (though it was in full use for decades previous). English Gothic in style, the Cathedral is built in the shape of a cross, complete with flying buttresses and gargoyles; but there are also 20th-century touches, such as a stained-glass window containing a piece of moon rock in honor of the flight of Apollo 11. The Cathedral was the setting for the funerals of Presidents Wilson (both he and his wife are buried here) and Eisenhower. At her request, Helen Keller and her companion, Anne Sullivan, are also buried here. The best way to see the Cathedral (if you still have the energy, otherwise save it for another day) is on a free one-hour tour; they leave continually, from the west end of the nave, Monday through Saturday from 10am to 3:15pm and Sunday from 12:30 to 2:45pm.

Winding Down   Just a bit farther north on Wisconsin Avenue, at Macomb Street, **Cactus Cantina** (tel. 202/686-7222) serves up traditional Mexican specialties made from fresh ingredients (you can watch tortillas being prepared near the entrance). Light streaming in through the windows, vintage photographs of Mexico, and festive colored lights make for a cheerful ambience. Weather permitting, you can sit outside at umbrella tables. The menu features moderately priced tacos, tamales, enchiladas, and fajitas, as well as mesquite-grilled chicken, pork ribs, shrimp, even quail. Mexican beers and pitchers of margaritas or sangria complement the menu. Cactus Cantina is open 11:30am to 11pm Sunday through Thursday, to midnight Friday and Saturday. *Note:* Other choices on this corner include Hunan and Thai restaurants.

GEORGETOWN

Start: 27th and Q Streets NW.

Directions: From Dupont Circle, take the D4 or D6 bus. Board at P Street between 20th and 21st Streets.

Finish: M Street near the Key Bridge.

Time: Approximately 4 to 6 hours, depending on stops and tours.

Best Times: Tuesday through Saturday, when you can do some of the suggested tours. It will be best to plan your arrival at Dumbarton House (Stop 1) in time for the 12:15pm tour. Then pace yourself to arrive at Tudor Place (Stop 9) in time for the 2:30pm tour (3pm on Saturday).

Georgetown was a thriving to-bacco and shipping port long before Washington, D.C., was formed. Originally a Native American village called Tohoga, it became part of the province of Maryland in 1700. Captain John Smith, believed to be the first white man to see the area in 1608, wrote in his *Historie of Virginie:* "The mildness of the aire, the fertilitie of the soil and the situation of the rivers are so propitious . . . no place is more convenient for pleasure, profit and man's sustenance. . . ."

The town of George—comprising 60 acres and named for the King of England—was officially established in 1751. It assumed new importance in 1790, when George Washington specified a nearby site on the Potomac for America's new capital city. It was incorporated into the District of Columbia in 1871. Today Georgetown is a charming upscale residential area, its tranquil tree-shaded brick and cobblestone streets lined with Georgian, Federal, and Greek Revival houses. The setting is just lovely for walking.

• • • • • • • • • • • • • • • •

Begin at:

1. **Dumbarton House,** 2715 Q Street NW. This Federal-style mansion, originally called Bellevue, was built between 1799 and 1805. It was moved 100 yards to its present location—in order to accommodate the nearby Dumbarton Bridge—in 1915. Since 1928, the house has served as headquarters for the National Society of Colonial Dames of America, who have furnished it with beautiful period antiques, including Hepplewhite, Sheraton, Chippendale, and Louis XVI pieces: A George III mahogany breakfront bookcase contains a full set of the Encyclopedia Britannica from 1797, and a painting by Charles Willson Peale is hung above a late-18th-century sideboard in the dining room. Past occupants of the house include the family of Joseph Nourse, first Register of the U.S. Treasury, and Charles Carroll, member of a prominent Maryland family. Noted architect Robert Mills, designer of the Washington Monument, was a boarder of the Nourse family. The entrance portico was designed by Benjamin Henry Latrobe, who also worked on the Capitol and the White House. Inside, the stunning entrance hall is adorned with a beautifully executed Adamesque frieze depicting arabesques and classical urns, and many of the rooms are embellished with exquisite moldings. A graceful stairway leads to a landing where light streams in from an arched Palladian window.

This is a stunning house, well worth touring. Free 30-minute guided tours are given Tuesday through Saturday between 10am and 1pm (last tour at 12:15pm). Call 202/337-2288 for details.

Turn right when you exit the house and right again at 28th Street, where you'll note:

2. **1607 28th Street NW,** the house occupied by Senator Edward Kennedy in the 1960s. Continue on to:

3. **Evermay,** 1623 28th Street NW, one of Georgetown's greatest mansions. It was built between 1801 and 1810 by Scottish real estate speculator and merchant Samuel Davidson. Something of an eccentric misanthrope, Davidson guarded his privacy by placing menacing ads in the daily papers informing "all sporting bucks with their dogs and guns" that his man Edwards was under orders to protect the property with the aid of "a good cudgel, tomahawk, cutlass, gun and blunderbuss, with powder, shots and bullets, steel traps, and grass snakes." The place is still fairly well fortified, and you can't go in, but do stand by the entrance gate and gaze.

    Follow the brick sidewalk and iron fence that run along:

4. **Oak Hill Cemetery,** founded in 1849 by banker/ philanthropist William Wilson Corcoran, whose collection formed the nucleus of the Corcoran Gallery of Art. He is buried here (in a Doric temple of a mausoleum), along with many other prominent Washingtonians, among them: John Howard Payne, composer of "Home Sweet Home" (his monument, topped by a bust, is to the right of the fountain on the front lawn); Edwin Stanton, Lincoln's secretary of war; and Dean Acheson, secretary of state under Truman. Corcoran purchased the property from George Corbin Washington, a great nephew of President Washington. It comprises 25 beautifully landscaped acres adjacent to Rock Creek Park, with winding paths shaded by ancient oaks. James Renwick, architect of the Smithsonian "Castle"— not to mention New York's St. Patrick's Cathedral and Grace Church—designed the iron enclosure and the Gothic-style stone chapel, the latter girded by graves of especially noted personages. The Victorian landscaping, in the Romantic tradition of its era, strives for a natural look (even the iron benches have a twig motif); in the same period style, many of the graves are symbolically embellished with inverted torches, draped obelisks, angels, and broken columns.

    Do take some time to stroll the grounds. You can purchase a map of graves at the gatehouse (3001 R Street NW), itself a beautiful brick-and-sandstone Italianate structure designed by George de la Roche in 1850. The cemetery is open Monday through Friday from 10am to 4pm, with the office closed for lunch between noon and 12:30pm. Visitors are requested to observe posted regulations. Note, as you exit, 2920 R Street, the beautiful house with a sweeping drive just across from the Oak Hill gatehouse: It's the home of *Washington Post* publisher Katherine Graham.

When you leave Oak Hill, continue on the brick pathway to your right. From here it's a pleasant stroll past Montrose Park to the area's most significant point of interest:

5. **Dumbarton Oaks,** 1703 32nd Street NW (with adjoining gardens around the corner on R Street). This Georgian mansion, built in 1800 and named for a Scottish castle, was the setting for the 1944 international conference that led to the formation of the United Nations. Past occupants Robert Woods Bliss and his wife, Mildred, turned over the estate and 16 acres (including 10 acres of exquisite formal gardens) to Harvard University (his alma mater) in 1940, along with an extensive collection of Byzantine art that included illuminated manuscripts, jewelry, sarcophagi, mosaics, icons, and more. In the 1960s, they also donated their pre-Columbian art collection to the complex and financed the building of two wings—one (designed by Philip Johnson) to house it, the other to contain Mrs. Bliss's library of gardening books. Pre-Columbian works (Olmec jade figures, funerary pottery, textiles, jewelry, sculpture) are displayed chronologically in an octet of glass pavilions. You can view museum exhibits, see the music room where the 1944 Dumbarton Oaks Conversations took place, and tour the magnificent formal gardens. Dumbarton Oaks additionally functions as a research center for Byzantine and pre-Columbian studies.

Dumbarton Oaks is open Tuesday through Sunday from 2 to 5pm (the gardens are open daily from 2 to 6pm from April 1 to October 31, daily from 2 to 5pm the rest of the year). Admission to the galleries is free; there is a charge to see the gardens.

Continue west along R Street to:

Georgetown

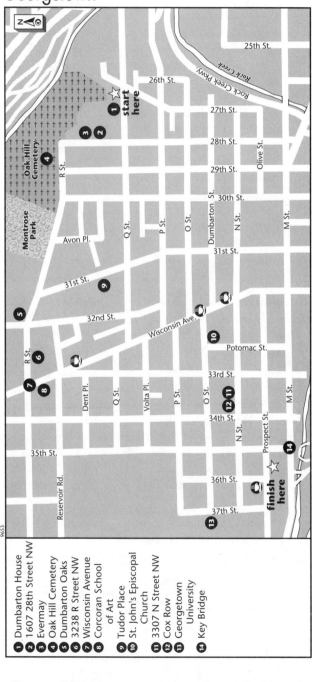

25th St.

Rock Creek

Rock Creek Pkwy.

26th St.

★ start here

27th St.

1

3 **2**

28th St.

Olive St.

4

29th St.

R St.

Oak Hill Cemetery

30th St.

Montrose Park

Avon Pl.

Q St.

P St.

O St.

Dumbarton St.

N St.

M St.

31st St.

9

31st St.

32nd St.

Wisconsin Ave.

5

10

Potomac St.

6

R St.

33rd St.

7

8

Dent Pl.

Q St.

Volta Pl.

P St.

O St.

12 **11**

M St.

34th St.

35th St.

N St.

Prospect St.

14

Reservoir Rd.

36th St.

finish here ★

13

37th St.

9653

1. Dumbarton House
2. 1607 28th Street NW
3. Evermay
4. Oak Hill Cemetery
5. Dumbarton Oaks
6. 3238 R Street NW
7. Wisconsin Avenue
8. Corcoran School of Art
9. Tudor Place
10. St. John's Episcopal Church
11. 3307 N Street NW
12. Cox Row
13. Georgetown University
14. Key Bridge

6. **3238 R Street NW,** an ivied early-19th-century Adams-style brick building with a Doric-colonnaded portico and a wealth of exterior detail, including decorative moldings. It was used as a summer White House by Ulysses S. Grant because its high elevation made it cooler than 1600 Pennsylvania Avenue. A less popular tenant was Union General Henry Wager Halleck, who, during the Civil War, enraged his neighbors (many of them Confederate sympathizers) by quartering soldiers in the house, using R Street as a drill field, and having a bugler sound reveille daily at dawn and taps at dusk.

   Turn left at:

7. **Wisconsin Avenue,** which, along with M Street, comprises Georgetown's commercial hub. Here, and on quieter side streets, you'll find numerous charming boutiques and antique shops.

   On your right, near Reservoir Road, is a Colonial-style brick building that houses the Georgetown branch of the:

8. **Corcoran School of Art,** 1680 Wisconsin Avenue NW, founded in 1890. It is the only professional school of art and design in Washington, D.C.

   Take a Break   The cozily charming **Café May Nay,** 1671 Wisconsin Avenue NW, just below Reservoir Road (tel. 202/338-5049), is a tearoom-like establishment with a beamed ceiling and gilt-framed oil paintings on the walls. Traditional Irish music complements menu items such as corned beef brisket, flavored with Guinness Stout, on rye with Dijon mustard. Salads and quiche are also options, and beverages include an Irish cream cappuccino. Everything is made from scratch. It's open daily from 11am to 7pm.

   Continue south on Wisconsin Avenue, make a left on Q Street and a left on 31st Street to:

9. **Tudor Place,** 1644 31st Street NW. This buff-hued stucco neoclassical mansion—the gem of all Georgetown houses—was designed by Dr. William Thornton, architect of the Capitol, and constructed between 1796 and 1816. Built for Georgetown mayor Thomas Peter (son of a Scottish tobacco and shipping magnate) and his wife, Martha Parke

Custis (step-granddaughter of George Washington), it remained in the Peter family for close to 200 years. After the last owner, Armistead Peter III, died in 1983, he left the house to the Tudor Place Foundation for public viewing; it opened its gates in 1988. Rooms are decorated to reflect various periods of the Peter tenancy. On a tour, note the stunning moldings in the parlors at either side of the entrance salon; both rooms are painted to reflect the Federal era. Another notable architectural feature is the circular portico that looks out on an expanse of lawn.

The house is rich in history. Prominent visitors included Robert E. Lee (who spent his last night in Washington in one of the upstairs bedrooms), Henry Clay, Daniel Webster, and John Calhoun. Many of the furnishings were inherited—or purchased at auction—from George and Martha Washington's Mount Vernon estate. On the tour, you can glance at a loving letter written by George Washington to his wife, Martha, dated June 18, 1775—right after he had been charged with the command of the Revolutionary Army by Congress: "My Dearest, I am now set down to write to you on a subject which fills me with inexpressable concern—and this concern is greatly aggravated and increased when I reflect on the uneasiness I know it will give you. It has been determined in Congress, that the whole Army raised for the defence of the American Cause shall be put under my care, and that it is necessary for me to proceed immediately to Boston to take upon me the Command of it … I should enjoy more real happiness and felicity in one month with you, at home, than I have the most distant prospect of reaping abroad, if my stay was to be Seven times Seven years. But, as it has been a kind of destiny that has thrown me upon this Service, I shall hope that my undertaking of it, is designed to answer some good purpose."

From the dining room window, Martha Peter and Anna Maria Thornton (wife of the architect) watched Washington burn during the War of 1812. One can only imagine the emotions felt by two women so directly involved in the formation of the capital city while helplessly observing its destruction. Thornton himself was at the Patent Office at the time, pleading—successfully—with the British not to burn it. A reception for the Marquis de Lafayette was held

in the drawing room in 1824. And during the Civil War—
the Peters were Confederate sympathizers (Robert E. Lee
was a friend and relative of the family)—to prevent the house
being appropriated for a Union hospital, they were forced
to rent rooms to Northern officers and their wives. Brittania
Peter Kennon's only stipulation was that they not discuss
the war in her presence. (Thomas and Martha Peter's daughters were rather grandly named: Columbia Washington,
America Pinckney, and Brittania Wellington).

Behind the house is a delightful five-acre Federal-period
garden with boxwood parterres, perennial flower beds,
statuary, a lily pool, bowling green garden, bird and lion
fountains, pear trees, vine-covered trellises, and intimate seating alcoves. A knot-pattern bed displays roses. Stroll through
the garden after your tour of the house; a self-guided map
is available. Comprehensive 45-minute house tours (a donation is requested) are offered Tuesday through Friday at
10am, 11:30am, 1pm, and 2:30pm; Saturday tours are given
on the hour between 10am and 3pm. Call 202/965-0400
for details.

When you leave Tudor Place, follow 31st Street South
to 0 Street and turn right, crossing Wisconsin Avenue and
proceeding for one block on the lower part of 0 Street en
route to:

10. **St. John's Episcopal Church,** Potomac and 0 Streets NW,
built in 1809. The church was partially designed by Dr.
William Thornton (see Stop 9 above). President Thomas
Jefferson contributed $50 toward the building fund; Dolley
Madison and the Minister to Great Britain (attended by
liveried servants with drawn swords) were among the leading parishioners, as were Tudor Place's Thomas and Martha
Peter; Francis Scott Key was a vestryman. The beautiful
stained-glass windows include one by Tiffany (it's the sanc-
tuary window to the right of the altar depicting *Easter Lilies
Crowned with the Gifts of God*). The parish office is open
weekdays from 9am to 4:30pm; if you ask, they'll open the
church for you to see. No one is on hand Saturdays; Sundays there are church services in the morning.

Take a Break **Sarinah,** 1338 Wisconsin Avenue
NW, at 0 Street (tel. 202/337-2955), offers first-rate

Indonesian fare. Among other items, the menu lists satays (skewers of lamb, beef, or chicken served with rice and peanut sauce), *gado-gado* (a vegetable salad served warm with rice in peanut sauce), and delicious soups (such as rice noodle in coconut milk with chicken, shrimp, hard-boiled egg, and vegetables). Sarinah's skylit, flagstone-floored interior, down a flight of steps from the street, sets tables amid a jungle of lush plantings; there are even trees growing through the ceiling. Prices are moderate. It's open for lunch Tuesday through Saturday from noon to 3pm.

A bit farther down the avenue is the chic and sophisticated **Paolo's,** 1303 Wisconsin Avenue NW, at N Street (tel. 202/333-7353), where tables spill out onto the street from an open-air patio. Its interior, with a stunning peach-hued Italian marble floor, centers on the warm glow of a pizza-oven fire. Entrées include pastas (such as thyme-infused raviolis filled with roasted eggplant and shiitake mushrooms), contemporary pizzas (perhaps brushed with jalapeño-lemon crème fraîche and topped with smoked Norwegian salmon, capers, and feta and taleggio cheeses), full dinner plates (such as jumbo shrimp scampi served with a crispy saffron risotto cake), and salads (on the order of pear and gorgonzola tossed with applewood-smoked bacon, roasted peppers, and raisins over mixed greens with red pepper aïoli). Prices are moderate. It's open for lunch daily from 11:30am through about midnight, and for Sunday jazz brunch from 11am.

Turn left at Potomac Street, right on N Street, and proceed to:

11. **3307 N Street NW.** John and Jacqueline Kennedy lived in this brick townhouse while he was a U.S. senator. It was purchased shortly after the birth of their daughter, Caroline. Across the street, at no. 3302, is a plaque (around the corner) inscribed by members of the press in gratitude for kindnesses received there in the days before Kennedy's presidential inauguration. Another plaque honors Stephen Bloomer Balch (1747–1833), a Revolutionary officer and a previous owner of the house.

Farther along N Street are five charming houses known as:

12. **Cox Row,** 3327–3339 N Street NW, built in 1817 and named for their owner/builder, Mayor of Georgetown (for 22 years) John Cox. He occupied the corner house at no. 3339; when Lafayette visited Washington in 1824 he stayed next door at no. 3337. Splendid dormer windows, Adam-style decoration on the facades, and handsome doorways are all characteristics of this Federal-period architecture.

Continue along N Street, observing the juxtaposition of Federal and Victorian styles (no. 3405 is particularly flamboyant) that makes Georgetown such an interesting study in architectural contrasts. Make a right on 37th Street to the campus of:

13. **Georgetown University,** 37th and O Streets NW. Founded in 1789, Georgetown is Washington's oldest university, the nation's first Catholic University, and the oldest American university run by Jesuits. Founder John Carroll (cousin of a Maryland signer of the Declaration of Independence) opened the university to "students of every religious profession." His close friends included George Washington (who, along with the Marquis de Lafayette, addressed students from "Old North") and Benjamin Franklin. After the Civil War, the university changed its colors to blue and gray to honor students slain in that conflict.

The campus is a beautiful one. As you enter, you'll be facing the eclectic Healy Building (1877–79), with its spires, towers, and gabled dormer windows (its architecture includes neo-Gothic, Medieval Revival, Victorian, Flemish Romanesque, and American Second Empire elements). The building is named for past president Patrick Healy, the first black American to head a major American university. If you have the energy, after all the walking we've done thus far, purchase a self-guided campus walking tour booklet in the bookstore at Leavey Center.

🍵 **Take a Break** **The Tombs,** 1226 36th Street and Prospect Street (tel. 202/337-6668), is a popular college hangout occupying a converted 19th-century house. It's innlike and cozy, with low ceilings, brick floors, and a working fireplace. The food—ranging from burgers, salads, and sandwiches to more substantial entrée specials, such as broiled salmon filet or a 14-ounce sirloin steak—is delicious and inexpensive. Open Monday through Friday from 11:30am, Saturday from 11am, and Sunday from 9am (Sunday brunch is served from 9am to 2pm).

From the university's front gate, make a right on 37th Street, and a left on Prospect Street. Make a right on 35th Street and follow it down to M Street, where you'll see the:

14. **Key Bridge,** named for Francis Scott Key, composer of "The Star-Spangled Banner." He once owned a house near the site. The bridge spans the Potomac River to Rosslyn, Virginia.

The C&O Canal, Including M Street

Start: M and 26th Streets.

Metro: Foggy Bottom; at the exit (there's only one), turn left on 23rd Street and walk to Washington Circle. Turn left again, crossing New Hampshire Avenue and K Street. Turn left onto Pennsylvania Avenue, and at 26th Street, turn right. Walk one block and turn left onto M Street. Or, make your life simple—take a taxi.

Finish: M and Potomac Streets.

Time: Approximately 3^1/$_2$ to 4 hours, not including lunch.

Best Times: Mornings, so that you can meander along the canal and not have to rush back before dark (the canal towpath is not lit). If you walk in the afternoon, plan to have dinner and take in a movie in Georgetown at the end of your stroll. This is a good choice for weekends, when many people are on the canal.

Note: If you don't mind carrying a picnic lunch, there are riverside picnic tables at Fletcher's Boathouse (Stop 15), where you can also purchase soft drinks.

∫till quaintly charming and faintly evocative of its colonial origins, M Street bustled with the activities of a thriving tobacco port through the late 1800s. A century later, it has evolved into one of the District's major shopping, restaurant, and club hubs, nightly prowled by restless hordes of Georgetown University students in search of action. As Georgetown's main drag, it is lined with small boutiques and antique shops punctuated by such well-known national emporia as J. Crew, Benetton, and Laura Ashley—not to mention Georgetown Park, an upscale mall of more than 100 shops with a flamboyantly Victorian interior.

Just a block south of M Street lies the fabled C&O Canal, which begins in Georgetown and parallels the Potomac River to Cumberland, Maryland, 184^1/$_2$ miles away. George Washington was the first to envision a water route through the Potomac Valley to the west. But actual construction didn't begin until 1828, when President John Quincy Adams turned the initial ceremonial spadeful of earth. From the first, canal construction was beset by problems: Labor was scarce, and indentured laborers from Europe had to be brought in; money ran out periodically; disease swept the labor camps; and there was fighting among different nationalities. The canal opened in 1831, at a time when water routes were still vital to trade and transportation. It was used to bring in manufactured goods from the east and carry coal from the west to the ports of the Atlantic Seaboard, for export to Europe and factories along the industrial tidewater. In its heyday, the only alternative to canal transport was expensive and inefficient horse-drawn vehicles (in one day four horses could carry a one-ton payload 12 to 18 miles, whereas using a canal towpath the same four horses could move 100 tons 24 miles per day). But the canal itself was rendered obsolete even as it neared completion; the infinitely more efficient B&O Railroad, constructed at the same time, was chugging along the identical Potomac route eight years before canal construction reached the Cumberland coalfields. After just a few decades, competition from rail and highway traffic—as well as flood damage—brought about the canal's decline and its eventual demise in 1924.

Though at the time the canal seemed to be a multi-million-dollar blunder, its capitulation to the industrial age has been a blessing to present-day Washingtonians. On its magnificent towpath—lined with ancient oaks, red maples, giant sycamores, willows, and wildflowers—one can leave urban cares and stresses behind while hiking, strolling, jogging, cycling, or boating. I've never hiked the canal without making a thrilling discovery—a proud mother duck with her new family in tow, raspberries suddenly abundantly in season, a brilliant flowering tree amid the greenery, a quaint canalside home, or a sudden appreciation of light shimmering on the water. And spring through fall, mule-drawn boats add a lyrical note to the canals attractions. (Plan a canal cruise for another time; they depart from the foot of Thomas Jefferson Street.)

This wonderfully scenic walking tour will cover four blocks of M Street, then double back to 30th Street to pick up the canal towpath and follow it 3.2 miles to Fletcher's Boathouse. You'll return along the same route, exiting at 32nd Street to link up with M Street for further exploration of Georgetown.

• • • • • • • • • • • • • •

Starting Out   For a luxurious prelude to your tour, stop in for breakfast at the elegant **Seasons** (in the Four Seasons Hotel), 2800 Pennsylvania Avenue NW (tel. 202/342-0444), where light streams in from a wall of windows overlooking the canal. Here, comfortably ensconced in a plush booth or neoclassic-design club chair, you can indulge in a delicious—albeit pricey—morning meal: perhaps gingered fruit bread French toast, fresh-baked croissants or brioches, poached eggs hollandaise with smoked salmon, or baked Shenandoah Valley trout with browned butter and pecans. Seasons opens for breakfast at 7am weekdays, 8am weekends.

Begin on M and 26th Streets at the:

1. **M Street Bridge,** which crosses Rock Creek, the Rock Creek Parkway, and the recreational trail that follows the creek. From here, proceed along the right side of M Street. You'll see plenty of typically tidy Georgetown sidestreets as you go along; anytime you feel the urge to explore one of them, feel free (or take the "Georgetown" tour in this book).

Between 28th and 29th Streets is the:

The C & O Canal, Including M Street

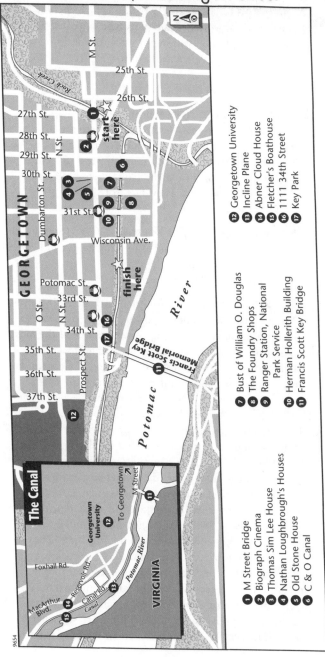

1 M Street Bridge
2 Biograph Cinema
3 Thomas Sim Lee House
4 Nathan Loughbrough's Houses
5 Old Stone House
6 C & O Canal

7 Bust of William O. Douglas
8 The Foundry Shops
9 Ranger Station, National Park Service
10 Herman Hollerith Building
11 Francis Scott Key Bridge

12 Georgetown University
13 Incline Plane
14 Abner Cloud House
15 Fletcher's Boathouse
16 1111 34th Street
17 Key Park

2. **Biograph Cinema,** 2819 M Street, which has been showing avant-garde and classic films here since 1965. Check out what's playing; you might want to sink into a movie seat after this considerable hike.

   Continue west on M Street. Across 30th Street (at no. 3001), you'll find the:

3. **Thomas Sim Lee House,** a single-family dwelling built by Lee, a Revolutionary patriot, delegate to the Continental Congress, and friend of George Washington. He was twice governor of Maryland, from 1779 to 1782 and 1792 to 1794. Lee also owned the land where buildings nos. 3005–3011 now stand. They date to 1810.

   Walk to:

4. **Nathan Loughbrough's Houses,** at 3039 M Street, built between 1801 and 1806, and restored by the Junior League of Washington in 1963.

   Next door, at 3051 M Street, is the:

5. **Old Stone House** (1766), the only surviving pre–Revolutionary War building in Washington. A private residence in the days when Georgetown was one of the most significant tobacco markets on the Atlantic seaboard, it stands on one of 80 lots surveyed in the port of Georgetown in 1751. Construction on it probably began in 1764; the front was finished in 1765, with the rear and second stories added later. The builder was Christopher Layman, a Pennsylvania-born cabinetmaker who lived here and maintained a shop on the premises. After his death, Layman's widow sold the house to Cassandra Chew, a prosperous businesswoman and socialite who raised two daughters here. Wealthier than the Laymans, the Chews listed slaves among their possessions. The house stayed in the Chew family through the early 1880s. From then until 1950, when the National Park Service took over the building, the Old Stone House served as a residence, a gun shop, a clockmaker's shop, a tailor shop, and a haberdashery. Rooms are furnished in 18th-century pieces. The front room is outfitted to represent Layman's workshop; his stack of pine planks, chisels, planes, and clamps are on display. Tours are self-guided, but park rangers in colonial attire are on hand to answer

questions. Occasionally, they give demonstrations of 18th-century homemaking skills, such as cooking on an open fireplace, candle dipping, spinning, or making pomander balls. Adjoining the house is a charming period garden bounded by a white picket fence. The house is open to the public Wednesday through Sunday from 9am to 5pm; admission is free.

☕ Take a Break If it's getting on toward lunchtime, make a small detour and head a few blocks west, making a right on Wisconsin Avenue. At N Street, you'll spot **Paolo's** (tel. 202/333-7353), a chic/simpatico California-style Italian restaurant where, in good weather, the facade is open-air and tables spill out on the street. The rose marble–floored interior, by contrast, centers cozily on the warm glow of a wood-burning pizza oven. Fare includes thin-crusted pizzas with toppings like oak-grilled chicken or goat cheese, great pastas, and more serious entrées such as a mixed grill of jumbo shrimp, sea scallops, medallion of beef tenderloin, and marinated chicken breast served with saffron risotto cake and fresh vegetables. Prices are moderate to high. Open Monday through Saturday from 11:30am, Sunday from 11am.

Cross to the opposite side of M Street, and return to 30th Street, a charming tree-lined Georgetown street, taking it south one block to the:

6. **C&O Canal,** where the towpath is bricked as far as 31st Street and then becomes a well-trodden dirt path. Turn right into the canal, where, on many days, walkers are outnumbered by cyclists and joggers.

When you enter the towpath, look on your right for a:

7. **bust of William O. Douglas,** whose efforts (see box above) resulted in the establishment of the C&O Canal Historic Park.

To your left, between 30th and Thomas Jefferson Streets, are:

8. **The Foundry Shops,** a complex of galleries and shops in a converted foundry beside the canal.

Further along on the opposite side of the canal is a:

9. **ranger station of the National Park Service,** where you can get maps and information about the canal.

At Thomas Jefferson Street, one of the most picturesque views of the canal, with trees overhanging it, comes into view. If you've brought your camera, this is a vintage shot. Jefferson once lived on this street.

The building on your right, at the corner across 31st Street, is called the:

10. **Herman Hollerith Building.** This is where the inventor, businessman, and "Father of Data Processing" perfected the punched-card tabulating machine, the forerunner to computer systems. In 1911 Hollerith, who worked for the

Justice for the Canal

Outdoor-loving Washingtonians should raise the occasional glass to conservation-minded Supreme Court Justice William O. Douglas, who served from 1939 to 1975. After flooding did serious damage to the C&O Canal and its towpath in 1924, ending its dwindling commercial usage, it was allowed to deteriorate. By 1954, there were plans to fill it in and build a scenic parkway along its route. Douglas led a fervent crusade to save the canal as a recreational facility, challenging pro-development news editors from the *Washington Post* to join him on a much-publicized eight-day hike along the entire length of the canal from Cumberland to Georgetown. Because of this crusade, the influential *Post* reversed its pro-highway stance, and preservation support grew. The parkway project was abandoned. In 1960, the canal was designated a national monument, and in 1971 it became a national park. Douglas, by the way, developed a passion for nature early on; he had polio as a child growing up in Washington State and regained the strength in his legs by hiking in the nearby Cascade Mountains. He authored 30 books, primarily about nature and conservation, including *Of Men and Mountains* (1950), *Beyond the High Himalayas* (1952), and *A Wilderness Bill of Rights* (1965). An annual 12-mile hike on the canal every April honors Douglas's walk.

Census Bureau, sold his company to the firm that would become IBM.

Continuing your walk, you'll pass a condominium complex with triangular patios, called the Flour Mill.

Take a Break **The Sea Catch,** at 31st Street (tel. 202/337-8855), offers waterside seating on an awninged wooden deck at a spot where mulberry and ailanthus trees form a verdant archway over the canal. While dining on seafood salads and fresh fish and seafood specials, you can watch ducks and punters gliding by. Inside, the dining areas are rustic, with random-plank oak floors, rough-hewn stone walls, and working fireplaces. Prices are moderate. Open for lunch Monday through Saturday from noon to 3pm, dinner from 5:30 to 10:30pm. *Note:* The Sea Catch also contains the last restrooms you'll pass for several miles.

Now look for a stairway leading to a pedestrian overpass; cross over to the other side of the canal here, since the side of the towpath you're on will end soon. Up ahead, you'll see a bridge with lampposts and a railing arching over the canal. It's the:

11. **Francis Scott Key Bridge,** named for the native son, lawyer, and author of "The Star-Spangled Banner," who lived nearby from 1805 to 1830. During the War of 1812, Key watched the bombardment of Fort McHenry in Baltimore from a ship in the harbor; the fiery siege continued throughout the night, but at dawn he was relieved to see the American flag still flying. The song he felt inspired to write was set to the tune of an old drinking song, "To Anacreon in Heaven." It became the national anthem in 1931.

The Whitehurst Freeway, which passes over the bridge and into Virginia, was engineered by partners Alexander and Repass in 1949. Repass was white and Alexander was African American, a racial and business accomplishment for the time. The two became friends when they played college football together in 1910.

You can check your watch by the clocktower visible here; the words "Car Barn" on the building refer to its original use in 1895, as a station for connecting streetcar lines.

After you walk under the Key Bridge, you'll get a good look at the Potomac River and the downtown towers of Rosslyn, Virginia, on the opposite side; among them are the offices of *USA Today* and Gannett publishers, and the Marriott Hotel.

Coming up on the right (look for steeples) is:

12. **Georgetown University,** established in 1789. The modern, rectangular building on the hill houses students and administrative offices. The two spires you see are part of the landmark Healy Building, named after Father Patrick Healy, a Jesuit priest and the first African American to receive a doctorate and serve as president (1873–82) of a predominantly white American university. Georgetown, by the way, is the alma mater of President Bill Clinton, who graduated in 1968.

When you come to traffic lights and signs for Canal and Foxhall roads, you'll take a wooden footbridge and see a spillway. The train track that you see is part of the now-defunct Georgetown branch of the Baltimore & Ohio Railroad; eventually the tracks will be taken up and the railroad bed converted to a bike path. Take a moment to turn around and admire the view of spires of the Healy Building one last time. From this point on, the city recedes, leaving you to relish the natural beauty of the canal.

In about a mile, you'll come to a marker, on the left, commemorating the:

13. **Incline Plane,** a system used to lower boats from the canal into the Potomac at this spot. The boats were eased one at a time into a bathtub-like contraption and lowered 300 feet at an angle into the river. The Incline Plane was built in 1875 to ease the frequent traffic jams, at a time when 500 boats a year used the canal. It was destroyed by a flood in 1889, as were miles of the canal itself, bankrupting the C&O Canal Company.

After you've walked another mile, you'll spot a small spillway; beyond it a couple of small bridges will come into view. The whitewashed stone house off to the right is the:

14. **Abner Cloud House,** built in 1799. Cloud also owned a nearby grain and flour mill and was a relative of the Pierce family, who owned a prosperous mill farther up the river,

which is now open to the public. Cloud died in 1812, so he didn't live to see the construction of the canal, but his wife, who died in 1852, did. The Cloud Mill closed in 1870. The house is usually closed to the public.

Across the canal from the Cloud House is a recreational and picnic area. It's also the site of:

15. **Fletcher's Boathouse,** where you can rent rowboats, canoes (for use on the canal only), and bicycles by the hour or the day. Fletcher's (tel. 202/244-0461) is open March to mid-November, daily from 7:30am to dusk. If you'd like to fish you can acquire a permit, bait, and tackle here. Bass, bluegill, perch, and catfish are plentiful, but if you catch an endangered or unusual fish, such as a trout, pike, pickerel, gar, walleye, or white shad, you're asked to return it to the water. There's a small concession stand at Fletcher's but choices are limited. Toilets are on the other side of the canal.

If you want to walk further, you can continue another mile and a quarter to the Chain Bridge, or rent a bike here and ride 14 miles to the historic Great Falls Tavern, now the main visitor center and a small museum for the C&O Canal National Historic Park. Otherwise, after you've rested, retrace your steps along the towpath back to Georgetown and exit at the rust-colored footbridge just after you pass under the Key Bridge. You'll be at 34th Street. As you ascend to M Street, note the shuttered white brick house on your right at:

16. **1111 34th Street,** with two horses' heads in the facade. Just across from it, on a brick landing, a marker tells you that this is the spot where Revolutionary General George Washington and French Army Commander-in-Chief Jean-Baptiste Rochambeau crossed the Potomac en route to Yorktown in September, 1781.

Across the way, just before M Street, is:

17. **Key Park,** a circular colonnaded brick plaza behind a rose garden. At its center is a bust of Francis Scott Key (1799–1843), lawyer, patriot, poet, and author of the song that became America's national anthem almost a century after his lifetime, in 1931. Among several informational plaques about Key here, one tells the story of the writing of "The

Star-Spangled Banner." Key was active in the antislavery movement and advocated the establishment of public schools. Between 1803 and 1833, his home and law office stood about 100 yards west of this park; a map shows you the exact location.

Winding Down Back on M Street, your dining choices are numerous. One of two excellent and moderately priced ethnic choices is **Aditi,** 3299 M Street NW (tel. 202/625-6825), a pristinely charming Indian restaurant where everything is made from scratch and uniquely spiced and sauced. Order up a platter of assorted appetizers, followed by an entrée of lamb biryani (an aromatic saffron- and rosewater-flavored rice pilaf tossed with savory pieces of lamb, cilantro, raisins, and almonds).

Or try another spicy cuisine—Ethiopian—at **Zed's,** 3318 M Street NW (tel. 202/333-4710), also pretty and cozy. Ethiopian food is eaten without utensils; dishes are scooped up in a sourdough crêpe-like bread called injera. I like the doro watt—chicken stewed in a tangy red-chili-pepper sauce; it comes with a hard-boiled egg that has been simmered in the same sauce. Order up a few side dishes with it—a purée of roasted yellow split peas, garlicky chopped collard greens, bulgur wheat blended with herbed butter, and marvelous potato and tomato salads.

If you don't want a full—or ethnic—meal, the best place for light fare is **Dean & Deluca,** a branch of the renowned fine food emporium, here occupying an 1865 markethouse with an awninged brick patio. Choices include scrumptious pastries with cappuccino, foccacia bread sandwiches, homemade soups, and salads. You can also buy appetizer portions of gourmet fare from the store and eat them in the café. Fine wines are available by the glass.

All three of the above-mentioned eateries are open daily for lunch and dinner.

THE NATIONAL ZOO & ROCK CREEK PARK

Start: Zoo entrance.

Metro: Woodley Park-Zoo. When you exit the Metro (there's only one exit) onto Connecticut Avenue, you'll see a bus stop, and beside it a sign pointing you toward the National Zoo. Walk a few blocks north (the street numbers get higher); the zoo is on the right side of the street.

Finish: P Street Bridge, P and 23rd Streets.

Time: Approximately 4 to 5 hours.

Best Times: At the zoo, mornings are best, so that you'll be there for the 11am panda feeding, which is often outdoors. (There is a second feeding at 3pm, but the panda is less active by then.) The zoo grounds are open daily from April 15 to October 15 from 8am to 8pm, the rest of the year, daily until 6pm; animal buildings are open 9am to 4:30pm daily year round.

The National Zoo—home to more than 5,000 animals comprising 500 species, many of them rare and/or endangered—occupies 163 verdant acres in northwest Washington along briskly flowing Rock Creek. When the zoo was established in 1889 "for the advancement of science and the instruction and recreation of the people," this part of Washington was undeveloped, except for a farmhouse or two. Both it and adjoining Rock Creek Park are woodsy regions, densely planted with towering oaks, maples, hickories, poplars, and sycamores. Renowned landscape architect Frederick Law Olmsted was its principal designer. In spring and summer zoo pathways are abloom with colorful annual and perennial flowers (many of them attracting butterflies), and hummingbirds flitter about the cactus garden beside the Small Mammal House. There are only two major paths in the zoo (together about 1½ miles), both extensively signposted so you can't get lost: Olmsted Walk passes by the habitat of Hsing-Hsing, a giant panda and the zoo's star resident, while the Valley Trail leads to exhibits themed on the Amazon River. The Zoo is part of the Smithsonian Institution.

Adjacent Rock Creek Park, in existence since 1890, was purchased by Congress for its "pleasant valleys and ravines, primeval forests and open fields, its running waters, its rocks clothed with rich ferns and mosses, its repose and tranquillity, its light and shade, its ever-varying shrubbery, its beautiful and extensive views." Under the auspices of the National Park Service, this idyllic landscape is one of the world's largest urban parks, encompassing a 1,750-acre valley in the District of Columbia and extending another 2,700 acres into Maryland. Much of it is still wild; it's not unusual to see a deer scurrying through the woods in more remote sections. Decades before it was designated a park, Abraham Lincoln took carriage rides through this magnificent greenbelt; Theodore Roosevelt often came here, sometimes with his children in tow, to fish, hike, and swim; and after he left the presidency in poor health, Woodrow Wilson found it pleasant to drive with his wife along Rock Creek's tree-shaded roadways. Today, the park is filled with Washingtonians at play—horseback riding, hiking, jogging, playing tennis or golf, picnicking, cycling, or simply enjoying the unspoiled natural setting.

• • • • • • • • • • • • • • • •

Starting Out If you're starting out early in the morning, have a pre-tour breakfast at **Animal Crackers,** 3000 Connecticut Avenue NW (tel. 202/667-0503), just across from the zoo entrance. This pleasant little self-service restaurant, with whimsical animal-themed prints on the walls, serves up a variety of bagels and cream cheese spreads, fresh-baked muffins and pastries, waffles, cherry-walnut cheesecake, hot chocolate, even fresh-squeezed orange juice. You can take a newspaper off the rack to read while you eat. In good weather, there's outdoor seating. You can also purchase picnic fixings here (sandwiches, salads, desserts) to eat in the zoo. Animal Crackers opens at 7:30am Monday to Friday, 8am Saturday and Sunday.

If, on the other hand, you'd like to begin after an early lunch, the place to go is **Petitto's,** just across from the Metro station at 2653 Connecticut Avenue NW (tel. 202/667-5350). Open for lunch weekdays from 11:30am to 2:30pm, this is one of Washington's best Italian restaurants. The menu features superb pastas such as pappardelle (wide fettuccine) mixed with chunks of sautéed chicken, exotic mushrooms, and prosciutto in a sage/marjoram/rosemary-flavored butter wine sauce. Marvelous salads are here, too, and desserts—most notably the tiramisù and the creamy orange cheesecake—are ambrosial. Petitto's is rather charming, occupying a turn-of-the-century townhouse with working fireplaces in each dining area. It, too, has umbrella tables on the street in warm weather. Prices are moderate.

This walk kicks off at the zoo, just inside the entrance to your left at the:

1. **Educational Building.** Pick up maps and find out about feeding times, where the current zoo babies are, and what activities are planned for the day. If you're going to a panda feeding, find out if it will be outdoors or in. There's also a large gift shop (the biggest and best in the zoo) and bookstore inside. It's run by FONZ, Friends of the National Zoo, which also runs the cafeteria and parking lots; proceeds go to the zoo.

Outside the Educational Building, directly across the path and nestled in a flower bed, is a:

2. **sculpture** carved from a fallen (and creatively recycled) willow oak. The stylized totem of animals and humans, by local artist Steven Weitzman, honors the many volunteers at the National Zoo and in the field of wildlife conservation. A sign in front of it lists daily zoo events.

From here, follow the blue Valley Trail a short distance to the:

3. **Wetlands Exhibit.** Follow the boardwalk to see a variety of ducks, herons, geese, brown pelicans, and other waterfowl that reside amid water lilies, water hyacinths, cattails, grasses, and wild rice. White pelicans, farther down the Valley Trail in another exhibit, are fun to watch at feeding time (the Educational Building staff can tell you when), as they grab the fish pitched to them by the zoo staff. They excel at snagging outside curves. Bald eagles live in an aviary here, and the delightful Bird House adjoins.

From the Wetlands Exhibit, head back along the boardwalk, turn right on Valley Trail, and turn left on Olmsted Walk where you'll pass swans en route to the:

4. **giant panda** Hsing-Hsing, who, with his companion Ling-Ling, was a gift from the People's Republic of China. They arrived here a couple of months after President Nixon's historic 1972 visit there (Ling-Ling died in 1992). Giant pandas are rare in zoos, as they are in the wilds. They're found only in the mountains of central China, where they live in dense bamboo and coniferous forests. Fewer than 1,000 remain in China, where the government has now set aside 11 protected nature preserves for them and imposed life sentences on those convicted of poaching. Though they do not hibernate, giant pandas are of the bear family. Hsing-Hsing's habitat consists of two big, interconnected play yards, each with wooden structures suggesting bridges, swings, and tree houses. He eats 20 to 40 pounds of bamboo a day and also enjoys apples. His habitat is, indeed, planted with bamboo, but only for decorative purposes; it is out of reach for nutritional ones. Lovely weeping willows further beautify Hsing-Hsing's home.

Just across from Hsing-Hsing is the outdoor habitat of the elephants and giraffes. If they're not outside, walk into the smelly:

The National Zoo

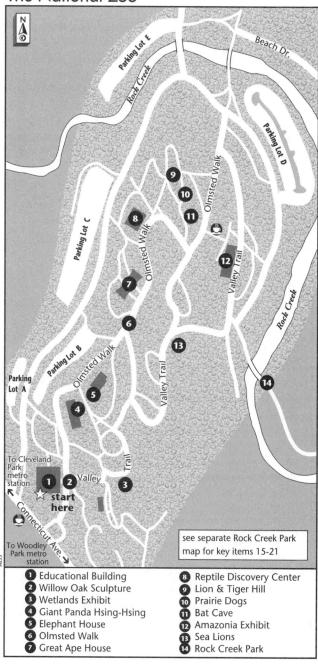

1. Educational Building
2. Willow Oak Sculpture
3. Wetlands Exhibit
4. Giant Panda Hsing-Hsing
5. Elephant House
6. Olmsted Walk
7. Great Ape House
8. Reptile Discovery Center
9. Lion & Tiger Hill
10. Prairie Dogs
11. Bat Cave
12. Amazonia Exhibit
13. Sea Lions
14. Rock Creek Park

see separate Rock Creek Park map for key items 15-21

5. **Elephant House,** which is also home to pygmy hippos and rhinos. The latter are in danger of extinction because the rhino's horn is prized for medicinal purposes and sells, in the Far East and other parts of the world, for thousands of dollars per pound. Rhinos are being bred here at the zoo, as are pygmy hippos (53 of them have been born here since 1931). Unlike river hippos, pygmy hippos spend much of

Birth of a Baby Elephant

Kumari, a star resident of the Elephant House, was the first elephant to be born at the zoo. She arrived December 14, 1993, weighing in at 264 pounds. Her 18-year-old mother, Shanthi, weighed 8,900 pounds by Kumari's delivery, having gained 1,000 pounds during her 22-month pregnancy! Shanthi had earned the right to a bit of compulsive overeating; she had a pretty traumatic childhood. Born in Sri Lanka, she was orphaned at a young age when her herd raided a village. As villagers chased the elephants away, Shanthi fell into a well, where a leopard attacked her. She was then reared at an elephant orphanage until 1977, when she was presented as a bicentennial gift from the children of Sri Lanka to the children of the United States. Her name means "peace," and Kumari's means "princess."

After Shanthi was selected for breeding, Elephant House curator John Lehnhardt visited every North American zoo with a breeding male Asian elephant to find her a suitable mate. He selected Indy, at the Burnet Park Zoo in Syracuse, New York; in 1991, Shanthi was taken to live there with him. She became pregnant early in 1992 and was returned to the National Zoo later that year. She had a remarkably easy delivery: Kumari was born in only 26 minutes, to the accompaniment of trumpeting and rumbling by delighted fellow Elephant House residents. Kumari's birth represents a ray of hope because wild Asian elephants, crowded by expanding human populations, are in serious danger of extinction—there are only about 40,000 left.

their time on land, roaming the forest. There are many interesting exhibits in this facility as well.

Outside the Elephant House entrance is:

6. **Olmsted Walk,** named for the zoo's designer, Frederick Law Olmsted, one of the greatest landscape architects of all time (and a personal hero of mine). Olmsted, who is best known for New York's Central Park, also created numerous other parks and greenspaces across the nation. Among them are the lush grounds surrounding the U.S. Capitol, which comprise a veritable arboretum with more than 200 species of trees and shrubs on display.

   Walk down the hill, past American bisons and the Small Mammal exhibit to the:

7. **Great Ape House,** where families of gorillas and orangutans live in close quarters. Mountain gorillas are an endangered species—as few as 310 may now exist—and zoos are working diligently to save them from extinction. Several have been born here in recent years. Adjoining the Ape House via an overhead Orangutan Transport System is the intriguing Think Tank, an exhibit about the biology and evolution of animal thinking. Here you can view orangutans and monkeys using tools, sending and receiving messages, employing social strategies, and otherwise showing off their innate cleverness. The Think Tank includes interactive exhibits, and trainer-assisted demonstrations take place several times throughout the day.

   Exit on the other side of the Ape House. Up ahead you'll see the:

8. **Reptile Discovery Center,** where you can view Indonesian Komodo dragons, the world's largest lizards (they actually do resemble dragons). Yet another endangered species, Komodo dragons are being bred here; Sobat, a female, and her mate, Friendty, have produced dozens of hatchlings, many of which have been raised at other zoos both in the United States and abroad. Also residing at the center are Burmese pythons, 12 to 15 feet long; a large, African softshell turtle that's been here since 1940; Cuban crocodiles; rhinoceros iguanas; and an array of snakes, turtles, and tortoises.

When you come out, walk left toward the gift shop, make another left at the zoo signs across the path, and proceed to the open moated enclosures of the:

9. **lions and tigers.** You may find the tigers tussling in the grass or swimming in the pond out front. They're one of the few cats that like being in water. Unlike lions, which live in prides on open plains, tigers are forest denizens.

Walk around this more or less circular habitat, exiting where you came in, and head left. You'll pass a mound of earth inhabited by:

10. **prairie dogs.** It's great fun to watch these little guys busily burrowing in and out of their holes, munching on carrots, sweet potatoes, apples, and corn. The American prairie dog population exploded when the West was settled and pioneers began killing off the coyotes, foxes, and bobcats that

---

The Komodo Dragon: No Mr. Nice Guy

Male Komodo dragons can grow to be 10 feet tall and weigh 200 pounds. Adults prey on deer, wild boar, monkeys, goats, dogs, even smaller Komodo dragons—they've been known to successfully tackle a 1,000-pound water buffalo by attacking and cutting the tendons of its leg. Protective coloring allows the dragon to hide itself in tall grasses; it can lunge forward with terrific speed to grab a passing animal. Like a snake, it can stretch the joints and movable bones of its jaw to encompass huge bites. An adult male can swallow a 33-pound boar whole, without even chewing—a feat similar to a human engorging a 20-pound turkey in a single gulp! Its teeth, about twice the size of a human's, are serrated and as sharp as a steak knife. Not a picky eater, the Komodo dragon will also devour putrefying carrion. Though the dragon is primarily a solitary animal, groups do gather at "meals," with smaller dragons showing deference to the larger, lest they anger the latter and end up as side dishes. Feeding also provides an opportunity for males and females to meet; it's not unusual for mating to occur at such gatherings. Quite the Roman orgy!

are their predators. However, it wasn't long before the settlers set out to exterminate the prairie dogs, which thrive on farm crops and pastures, themselves.

When you've had enough of the prairie dogs, take the semicircular path opposite the Mane Restaurant (look for marker no. 22) that leads to the:

11. **Bat Cave,** a small, fascinating exhibit built into the hillside. The supersonic creatures whiz back and forth, stopping to grab a bite from hanging fruits—cantaloupe, watermelon, and bananas. The bats attach themselves upside down to the ceiling to enjoy their snack, to snooze, or to stretch their wings. Few people know that almost a quarter of the mammal species are various kinds of bats; they live everywhere except the polar regions and some remote islands.

Take a Break   Occupying a stone house, the **Mane Restaurant** is a pleasant plant-filled cafeteria with windows overlooking lush foliage and walls hung with photographs of zoo animals. There are picnic tables outside. Light fare—burgers, grilled chicken sandwiches, chili, salads, and soups—is offered.

Past the Mane Restaurant, turn right on the Valley Trail and head for the:

12. **Amazonia Exhibit,** a rain forest habitat which includes a cascading tropical "Amazon River." Housed in a futuristic glass-domed building, it is home to 358 species of plants and dozens of animals. Visitors enter a "flooded forest" where the interrelatedness of life in the rain forest is stressed. Hummingbirds, monkeys, and frogs flit about the flooded trees, which are festooned with orchids and vines; a variety of fish swim in the waters. A villager's hut and a child's canoe are reminders that humans, too, are part of this environment. Murals depicting the Amazon's delta enhance the exhibit's verisimilitude, and its educational value is furthered by interactive displays. Immense naturalistic aquariums simulate deep river pools. After exploring the "field station" of "eccentric scientist" Dr. Brasil, you'll enter the actual rain forest, where the humidity and temperature rise, and chirping tanagers and red-crested cardinals dart from branch

to branch of mahogany, kapok, and balsa trees. Vines stretch toward the sunlight streaming in from the 50-foot glass dome, and water cascades over rocks into quiet river pools.

From here, continue past Amazonia and walk uphill, past the spectacled bear, to see the:

13. **sea lions** cavorting, amusing themselves and their human admirers by diving, surfacing, bellowing, and zipping underwater in their pool. Upstairs, the pool is bordered by a trellised walkway.

Retrace your steps towards Amazonia and look for a small bridge right before it. Cross the bridge, and turn right on the first asphalt path. You are now in the unspoiled and tranquil precincts of:

14. **Rock Creek Park,** its pristine beauty yet another tribute to Frederick Law Olmsted, who urged Congress to safeguard this vast greenbelt as "a pleasuring ground for the benefit and enjoyment of the people of the United States." The lushly planted path, adjacent to the meandering creek, on which you're walking is a popular jogging and bike route. You'll be following it as far as the P Street Bridge, near Dupont Circle, a good hour's walk.

Keep an eye out for the marker indicating the:

15. **site of Adams Mill,** one of seven mills that used to operate along Rock Creek in the 18th and 19th centuries. Two mills have stood at this site. The second one is named for President John Adams, who had a financial investment in it; however, because it was poorly sited on the creek, he lost money. The mill shut down in 1867.

Here the creek broadens. Follow the path until you are standing on a:

16. **small bridge,** admiring two striking arched ones to your right beyond it. They are the **Calvert Street Bridge** (renamed the Duke Ellington Bridge), built in 1935 and embellished with sculptures symbolizing air, rail, ship, and highway travel; and the ornate beaux-arts 1906 **William Howard Taft Bridge,** which Connecticut Avenue passes over. This is a particularly pretty spot, with trees reflected in the creek.

Rock Creek Park

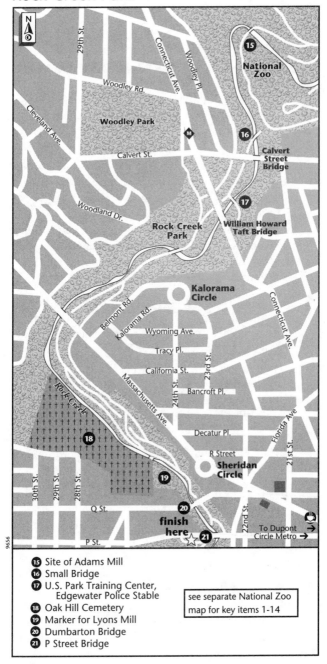

National Zoo

Woodley Park

Rock Creek Park

Kalorama Circle

Sheridan Circle

Calvert Street Bridge

William Howard Taft Bridge

finish here

To Dupont Circle Metro

15 Site of Adams Mill
16 Small Bridge
17 U.S. Park Training Center, Edgewater Police Stable
18 Oak Hill Cemetery
19 Marker for Lyons Mill
20 Dumbarton Bridge
21 P Street Bridge

see separate National Zoo map for key items 1-14

Turn right on the sidewalk along the parkway and follow the path under the arch of the Calvert Street Bridge.
On your left up ahead, you'll notice a sign for the:

17. **U.S. Park Training Center, Edgewater Police Stable,**
where the park police keep their horses. Soon after you walk
under the second (Taft) bridge, you'll cross a road and come
immediately upon the beginning of a 1.5-mile exercise trail
with 28 calisthenics stations. The trail winds downhill here,
and, as you follow it, you'll notice planes passing overhead
en route to National Airport. The trail switches places with
the creek again and passes over it. The creek is now on your
right side. You'll pass four more exercise stations. For the
next stretch of the walk, the trail is tightly wedged between
the parkway and the creek. The woods along here are filled
with vine-draped trees and branches overhanging the creek.
After a considerable walk, you'll pass another group of exercise stations. Here glance up, across the creek, at the:

18. **Oak Hill Cemetery,** which was founded in 1849 by
banker/philanthropist William Wilson Corcoran, who is
buried here. For further details on the cemetery, see Stop 4
in Walking Tour 7, "Georgetown."

At this point in the tour, except for parkway traffic, it's
easy to forget you're in a city. At the edge of the cemetery,
cross a small bridge. The creek will now be on your left,
and the path will lead you away from the parkway. To your
left, at the end of the bridge, is a:

19. **marker for Lyons Mill.** The mill, established in 1780
and in operation until 1875, stood near here and was perhaps the most successful venture on the creek. It covered
65 acres that included a barn, smokehouse, icehouse,
carriage house, stable, two stone houses, and the mill
itself, made of brick, stone, and wood—all of which have
vanished with time.

Soon the:

20. **Dumbarton Bridge** rises into view. Also known as the
Buffalo Bridge, it was built in 1914 to connect Georgetown
with the Kalorama area. The bridge has five striking
Renaissance-style arches and is adorned with depictions of
the faces of Native Americans made from a life mask of

Sioux Chief Kicking Bear; the sculptor was A. P. Proctor. Note the buffaloes at either end.

Walk under the bridge. Almost immediately, you'll see the:

21. **P Street Bridge,** at P and 23rd Streets NW. To get to P Street, follow the road veering to the right and take the wooden steps in the hillside to your right. Continue on P Street towards the Dupont Circle Metro and area restaurants.

Winding Down The Dupont Circle area abounds with restaurant choices. On P Street (no. 2121), you'll come directly to **Gabriel,** in the Radisson-Barceló Hotel, (tel. 202/293-3100), serving first-rate tapas and other culinary specialties of Spain and Mexico (see details in Walking Tour 6, "Embassy Row").

Or, if the weather is fine, consider the plant-filled **D.C. Café,** 2035 P Street (tel. 202/887-5819), which has umbrella tables out on the sidewalk. Open 24 hours, it serves up inexpensive Middle-Eastern specialties such as pita sandwiches stuffed with tahini and fried eggplant, falafel platters, gyros, tabouleh salad, moussaka, or kefte kebabs (Mediterranean charbroiled meatballs served with rice and salad). Less exotic fare includes burgers, American sandwiches, pizzas, buffalo wings, and subs. The homemade baklava makes a great dessert.

ARLINGTON NATIONAL CEMETERY

Start: Entrance to Arlington Cemetery

Metro: Arlington Cemetery.

Finish: Arlington National Cemetery Information Center.

Time: Approximately 3 to 4 hours.

Best Times: Try to start at 8am, when the cemetery first opens; the crowds start to arrive by 9:30am. If early rising is anathema to you, however, don't worry; it's only at the Kennedy graves that crowding is a problem.

You might wonder how a single cemetery could consume several hours of your time—but this is no ordinary cemetery. Arlington National Cemetery, the final resting place for more than 225,000 Americans who have served their country in the armed forces (as well as their spouses and children), covers 612 acres, contains 16 miles of roads, and encompasses more than 200 years of American history.

The cemetery land was originally part of Gen. Robert E. Lee's 1,100-acre estate, inherited by his wife from her parents. When

Lee resigned his army post and took command of the Confederate Army, Union troops took over the house; in 1864 some 200 acres of Lee's land were set aside for a national cemetery. The first burials here were in that same year, from fighting that took place in Virginia.

Burial was by rank and race here until 1948, but now the grave of a private may lie beside that of a general. Today there are 90 to 100 burials a week at Arlington, and the cemetery is expected to be full to capacity by the year 2025.

A visit to Arlington affords time for retrospection, an opportunity to remember the lives of those lost on the battlefield, and a startlingly beautiful vista of Washington.

A first visit here can be overwhelming because the cemetery is so vast, so a tour is especially helpful. There are no restaurants in or near the cemetery, nor can you have a picnic within its grounds, so eat a hearty breakfast before you embark on this walk.

Arlington National Cemetery is open to visitors daily April through September from 8am to 7pm, until 5pm the rest of the year. Call 703/692-0931 for further information.

● ● ● ● ● ● ● ● ● ● ● ● ● ● ● ●

When you exit the Metro, you'll see Arlington's Memorial Gate in front of you. On the hill above it is Arlington House, the former home of Gen. Robert E. Lee and his family. Behind you is the:

1. **Arlington Memorial Bridge,** a symbol linking the North, represented by the Lincoln Memorial, and the South, represented by Arlington House. On January 16, 1932, President Herbert Hoover dedicated the bridge, along with Memorial Drive, which leads to the cemetery gates, and the impressive entrance to the cemetery itself.

   In front of the bridge, to your right, is a statue known as:

2. **The Hiker.** It's the United Spanish War Veterans Memorial, placed here in 1965. A lone soldier stands atop a base with an inscription naming the arenas of that war, fought from 1898 to 1902: Cuba, Puerto Rico, the Philippines, and the United States.

   Across the road from it stands the:

3. **Seabees Memorial.** The U.S. Naval Construction Battalion (or "C.B.," thus Seabees) was formed early in World War II to build and defend bases to be used by combat forces. The statue in front depicts a soldier holding the hand of a child. Part of the quote on the bas-relief behind them states " . . . the difficult we do at once; the impossible takes a bit longer." The sculptor, Felix de Weldon, also created the nearby sculpture of Admiral Byrd as well as the Iwo Jima Memorial.

As you walk toward the cemetery, you will see the modern:

4. **Information Center** on your left. Here you can view exhibits and get a map, information, books, videos, and tickets for the Tourmobile, which threads through the cemetery every 15 minutes, stopping first at the Kennedy gravesites, then the Tomb of the Unknowns, and finally Arlington House. You can hop on and off it as often as you please, so if you think you might get weary of walking (the first half of the walk is uphill), the fare is a good investment. Tickets are sold only here. The bookstore in the Information Center sells the excellent book *Arlington National Cemetery—Shrine to America's Heroes* by James Edward Peters, and the compelling video "Arlington National Cemetery—A Video Salute to America's Heroes," which relives the history of Arlington and captures its beauty in each of the four seasons (for mail order, call toll free 800/783-5564). Consider using the restroom facilities here; there are no others until you come to Arlington House (Stop 21).

After visiting the Information Center, return to the main road for the most dramatic entry into the cemetery. Directly across the street from the Information Center is a:

5. **statue of Rear Adm. Richard Byrd, Jr.** (1888–1957), erected by the National Geographic Society. Byrd, a recipient of the Congressional Medal of Honor, was an aviator and explorer who flew over both the North and the South Poles and made five expeditions to Antarctica. He is buried in Section 2 of Arlington Cemetery, under a regulation headstone.

You'll also pass monuments honoring the exploits of the 101st Airborne Division ("The Screaming Eagles") and all of America's armored forces.

Walk straight ahead, and enter the cemetery, on your right, through:

6. **Schley Gate,** named after Rear Adm. Winfield Scott Schley (1839–1909), who led American troops to victory in Santiago Harbor, Cuba, in 1898, during the Spanish-American War. Opposite it is the **Roosevelt Gate,** named for Theodore Roosevelt. On the lawn between the two gates there eventually will be a memorial to all the women who have served in the armed forces.

    As you enter the cemetery, remember to stick to the designated paths and stay off the grass (if you are handicapped or have family buried here, you can get a special pass), and refrain from eating as long as you are on cemetery grounds.

    Take the first path to the right, and walk down the steps. Opposite the fourth step from the bottom, to your right, you'll see a simple marker, no. 36-1431, that designates the:

7. **grave of Medgar Evers** (1925–63), field secretary of the National Association for the Advancement of Colored People (NAACP) in Mississippi. Evers, who participated in the Normandy invasion on D-Day, for which he was awarded two Bronze Stars, was killed outside his home in Jackson, Mississippi after a civil rights rally.

    From his grave, return to the main road. On the other side of it, you'll see two sets of stairs leading up a hill. In between the two, but closer to the right stairway, is the:

8. **grave of Gen. Omar Nelson Bradley** (1893–1981), the last of America's five-star generals, who in World War II led the largest American force ever assembled, the Twelfth Army Group. Bradley succeeded Dwight Eisenhower as Army Chief of Staff in 1948 and soon became chairman of the Joint Chiefs of Staff. He became a five-star general, one of only five people ever to hold that rank.

    Continue along this right-hand terra-cotta-hued path. The large old oak tree beside the road here is about 400 years old. At the top of the path is the 14$^1/_2$-foot-high rose granite marker for the:

9. **grave of President William Howard Taft** (1857–1930) and his wife. Taft was the only president to serve on the Supreme Court (he was Chief Justice from 1921 to 1930); he also was the first civilian governor of the

Arlington National Cemetery

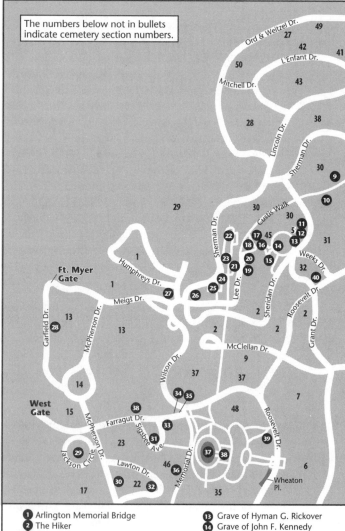

The numbers below not in bullets indicate cemetery section numbers.

1. Arlington Memorial Bridge
2. The Hiker
3. Seabees Memorial
4. Information Center
5. Statue of Rear Admiral Richard Byrd, Jr.
6. Schley Gate
7. Grave of Medgar Evers
8. Grave of Gen. Omar Nelson Bradley
9. Grave of President William Howard Taft
10. Tomb of Robert Todd Lincoln
11. Weeks Memorial
12. Graves of Potter Stewart and Thurgood Marshall
13. Grave of Hyman G. Rickover
14. Grave of John F. Kennedy
15. Grave of Robert F. Kennedy
16. Grave of Allard Lowenstein
17. Grave of Mary Randolph
18. Lookout Point
19. Grave of Pierre Charles L'Enfant
20. Grave of Brigadier General Horatio Wright
21. Arlington House
22. Robert E. Lee Museum

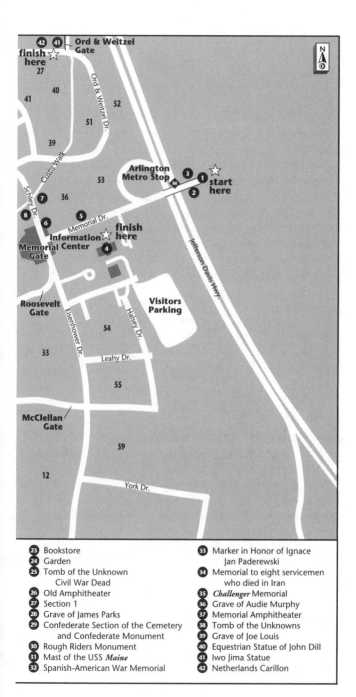

42 Netherlands Carillon
41 Iwo Jima Statue
finish here
27 Section 1

Ord & Weitzel Gate

40 Equestrian Statue of John Dill
41
52
51
39

Ord & Weitzel Dr.

Custis Walk

53

Arlington Metro Stop

3 **1** ☆ **start here**
M
2

7
36

8 Schley Dr.
6
5
Memorial Dr.

☆ **finish here**

Information Center
4

Memorial Gate

Jefferson Davis Hwy.

Roosevelt Gate

Visitors Parking

Eisenhower Dr.

Halsey Dr.

54

33
Leahy Dr.

55

McClellan Gate

59

12
York Dr.

Philippines, from 1900 to 1904, and was Secretary of War under Theodore Roosevelt. Taft served as president from 1909 to 1912; by that time he weighed over 300 pounds and couldn't fit into the White House bathtubs (he had to order the installation of a special giant-size tub in the executive mansion). Taft was also the first president to toss the first baseball of the season, starting a long-standing tradition. Helen Taft, the only first lady buried in Arlington Cemetery, deserves praise for bringing the famous cherry trees to Washington.

From the Taft grave, return to the road and backtrack a few steps to follow the other stairway and Custis Walk. Near the top of the steps, in a grove of holly trees to your left, is the granite:

10. **tomb of Robert Todd Lincoln** (1848–1926), eldest son of Abraham Lincoln. His wife, Mary Harlan (1846–1937), and son, Abraham Lincoln II (who died at age 17) are also interred here. Robert Todd Lincoln was part of Gen. U. S. Grant's staff during the Civil War. After the war, he became a lawyer and was appointed Secretary of War by President James Garfield, and was Minister (Ambassador) to Great Britain from 1889 to 1893. He was president of the Pullman Company of Chicago from 1897 to 1911. There were many ironies in Robert Todd Lincoln's life. He was the only child of Abraham and Mary Todd Lincoln who survived to adulthood, and as a young man was saved from falling in front of a train by Edwin Booth, the brother of the man who would assassinate his father. He also witnessed the assassinations of two other American presidents, Garfield, in 1881, and McKinley, in 1901. He never aspired to the presidency himself, with good reason.

Continue in the same direction along Custis Walk (it takes its name from the original owners of Arlington House) and turn left when you get to a paved road. Down a ways on your right, you'll notice a large semicircular granite:

11. **monument marked "Weeks."** This is the resting place of John Wingate Weeks (1860–1926), who served as both a congressman and senator from Massachusetts and was Secretary of War under Warren G. Harding and Calvin Coolidge.

Up on the lawn behind the Weeks Memorial is the:

12. **grave of Potter Stewart** (1915–85), associate justice of the Supreme Court from 1958 to 1981 and a lieutenant in the Navy during World War II. He was succeeded on the high court by Sandra Day O'Connor, the first female justice.

    Next to Stewart is the **grave of Thurgood Marshall** (1908–93), who was the first black Supreme Court justice.

    Behind Stewart's marker, to the right, is that of:

13. **Hyman G. Rickover** (1900–86) and his two wives. Rickover was an innovative naval scientist whose work propelled the Navy into the nuclear age with the 1954 launching of the *Nautilus,* the world's first nuclear-powered submarine. Hard-working and energetic, Rickover retired from the Navy at age 82—at the Navy's suggestion—and lived in the city of Arlington until his death four years later. Hyman Rickover immigrated with his family to the United States from Czarist Russia when he was six years old.

    Take the first right (or just follow the crowd) and follow the curving granite walkway up the hill to the:

14. **grave of John F. Kennedy** (1917–63), the most visited grave in Arlington Cemetery. At the entry is an oval area with a low wall inscribed with seven quotes by the fallen president, including "Let the word go forth from this time and place . . . that the torch has been passed to a new generation of Americans." Kennedy, the nation's 35th president, used to love to come to Arlington House and gaze out at Washington; only 12 days before he was assassinated he came here and said, "I could stay here forever." For this reason, Jacqueline Kennedy chose the burial site at the base of the house for his final resting place. The eternal flame was lit by Mrs. Kennedy toward the end of her husband's burial service at Arlington, on November 25, 1963, three days after his assassination. Two of the President's and Mrs. Kennedy's children, who died in infancy and were buried in Boston, were reinterred on either side of their father on December 4, 1963. They are an unnamed daughter who was born and died August 23, 1956 and a son, Patrick Bouvier Kennedy (August 7–August 9, 1963). In May 1994,

Jacqueline Bouvier Kennedy Onassis (1929–94) was buried here; you'll see her marker next to her husband's.

As you face John Kennedy's final resting spot, to the left is the path leading to the:

15. **grave of Robert F. Kennedy** (1925–68), his brother, marked by a simple white wooden cross on the hillside beneath Arlington House. Opposite the grave is a fountain with quotes from two of Robert Kennedy's speeches against oppression, one given in South Africa in 1966, and the other, denouncing racial division within the United States, given in Indianapolis in 1968. Robert managed the successful congressional and presidential campaigns of his older brother, John. Under JFK, he served as attorney general. After his brother's death, he sought national office, first as a senator from New York, and then as a candidate for the Democratic presidential nomination. It was during this campaign that he was killed in Los Angeles on June 5, 1968. Robert Kennedy died at age 43 (his brother's age when he became president of the United States).

From here, walk back through the oval fronting John Kennedy's grave and take the short walkway leading up the hill beside it. To the right you'll see the:

16. **grave of Allard Lowenstein** (1929–80), with a single quote on the tombstone: "If a single man plant himself on his convictions and there abide, the huge world will come around to him." Lowenstein was a lawyer, congressman from New York, and civil rights proponent.

Return to the main road and retrace your steps to Custis Walk. Turn left onto it and follow the long graded steps up the hill. As you near the top of the hill, to the left, you'll see a marker in front of a grave enclosed by a brick wall. Here lies:

17. **Mary Randolph** (1762–1828), the first person to be buried at Arlington. A direct descendant of Pocahontas, she was a cousin of Thomas Jefferson and Robert E. Lee. Her enigmatic epigraph, proclaiming that she died "a victim to maternal love and duty," was written by her son, crippled in adulthood, whom she cared for until her death.

From here take the side path to the left to a:

18. **Lookout Point,** which affords the best view of John F. Kennedy's grave. The only building you see today that the Lee family would have seen as they gazed outward from here in the mid-19th century is the Capitol, the first wing of which was erected in 1800; at that time it had a copper dome. In 1855 the dome you see now was begun.

    Proceed to the top of the hill for an even loftier view. Here, you can see that the Kennedy grave lines up exactly with the Memorial Bridge and the Lincoln Memorial. To the right of the flagpole is the:

19. **grave of Pierre Charles L'Enfant** (1754–1825), overlooking the city he planned in 1791 at the behest of George Washington. If you had a bird's-eye view of the monument over his grave, you'd be able to see that his original design for the city embellishes the top of it. A Frenchman, L'Enfant decided to join in the American Revolution at age 22; afterward, he lived in New York City. As the head architect for building the new capital, L'Enfant had several fallings out with the city fathers and lost his job within a year of his appointment. His design was still used, since his assistant, Benjamin Banneker, had an excellent memory. L'Enfant died penniless and forgotten in Maryland. His remains were moved here in 1909; he is one of 11 Revolutionary War soldiers who have been reinterred in Arlington Cemetery. The beautiful city of Washington owes him a great debt.

    To the left of the flagpole lie the remains of:

20. **Brig. Gen. Horatio Wright** (1820–99), a Civil War hero and the chief of army engineers. He was responsible for bringing the construction of the Washington Monument to completion in 1884. He also commanded troops that successfully defended Washington against Confederate attacks during the Civil War.

    Atop the hill stands the stately:

21. **Arlington House,** built by Robert E. Lee's father-in-law, George Washington Parke Custis. He was the son of Martha Custis Washington, and was adopted by George Washington and raised at Mount Vernon. Custis's only child, Mary, fell in love with a dashing young army officer

named Robert E. Lee, a distant cousin she had known since childhood (they fell in love when they were teenagers). They were married in a military-style wedding in the front parlor of the house on June 30, 1831. The couple lived here with the Custises and inherited the estate at their death. Six of their seven children were born here.

Robert E. Lee left his beloved home forever on April 22, 1861, when he accepted the command of the Confederate forces after his home state, Virginia, seceded from the Union. One month later, it was occupied by Union troops; officers used the house and thousands of soldiers were quartered on the property. Some 200 acres of virgin oak forest behind the house was cut for firewood and bases for tents and two earthenworks forts.

In 1882, the U.S. Supreme Court returned the estate to Robert E. Lee's eldest son, Washington Custis Lee, but with thousands of graves surrounding the house, he could not live in it. Lee sued the federal government, which, in a case that went all the way to the Supreme Court, was forced to buy the land for $150,000.

Arlington House was dedicated in Robert E. Lee's honor by Congress in 1925, and in 1955 it was made a permanent memorial to him. Today park rangers dressed in period costume greet you at the door, answer questions, and offer you a self-guided tour (be sure to pick up a tour brochure at the entrance) through the house: You can see the parlors downstairs (the green furniture in the white parlor, some of the red furniture, and a portrait of Mrs. Lee in the opposite parlor are original to the house) and bedrooms upstairs (walk in a clockwise direction to see the girls' sleeping quarters, the older sister's room that was shared with a cousin, the boys' room, and the Lees' bedroom, where Lee decided to resign from the U.S. army).

In the North Wing, you'll see the winter kitchen, the wine cellar, and the room where sewing was done (and where Mrs. Custis and later Mrs. Lee taught their slaves to read and write). There were 63 slaves on the property before the Civil War, and Mr. Custis stipulated in his will that they be freed within five years of his death; in 1863 Robert E. Lee officially freed all the slaves at Arlington House.

An American Dynasty: The Lees of Virginia

The history of one of the state's most noted families begins with Richard Lee, born in Shropshire, England, in 1613. As a younger son, his prospects were poor; so, after some legal and business education in London, he emigrated to Virginia in 1639 to serve as Clerk of the Quarter Court at Jamestown and to engage in fur trading. In 1649, Lee was appointed colonial Secretary of State. He frequently traveled to London in the interests of trade, became a successful planter, and amassed a vast fortune.

Many of Richard's descendants played major roles in American history. Richard Henry Lee (1732–94) and Francis Lightfoot Lee (1734–97) were signers of the Declaration of Independence. As a Virginia senator and a leader in the Continental Congress, Richard Henry proposed that "these United Colonies are, and of right ought to be, free and independent States." He was also influential in the adoption of the Bill of Rights.

Henry Lee (1756–1818), known as "Light Horse Harry," was a Revolutionary hero and a friend of George Washington. He played a leading part in the Virginia convention that ratified the Federal Constitution and served as governor of Virginia and in Congress. He penned the historic eulogy for George Washington: "First in war, first in peace, and first in the hearts of his countrymen."

Light Horse Harry was also the father of the most famous Lee—General Robert E. Lee (1807–70). As a loyal Virginian—though opposed to both slavery and secession— Lee resigned his Army commission when the state seceded in 1861. He had spent 32 years protecting the Union, and was Lincoln's choice to command Northern forces. However, after an agonizing personal struggle, Lee decided that he could not take up arms against his fellow southerners. On April 22, 1861 he assumed the rank of Major General of Virginia's military forces. In February of 1865—just two months before he surrendered at Appomattox—Lee was named general-in-chief of the Armies of the Confederate States.

You'll exit at the rear of the house and walk around back to the North Wing, passing the house's original well and a massive cedar tree that was planted here in 1872.

Exit the North Wing, turn right, pass the house's restored vegetable garden, and visit the small:

22. **museum,** devoted to Robert E. Lee's family history (his father was a congressman and a three-term governor of Virginia, and two of his cousins signed the Declaration of Independence) and the course his life took after he left Arlington House (Lexington, Virginia, would become his home after the Civil War until his death). Among the items on display are Lee's mess kit, the key to the tomb of the Unknown Soldiers of the Civil War, and locks of Lee's hair and of his favorite horse Traveller's mane.

From here, walk to the:

23. **bookstore** behind the main house, where you'll find an extensive collection of books. (There is a large bookstore in the Visitors Center, as well, so you don't have to carry purchases with you for the rest of your walk.)

From here, take a minute to look at the:

24. **garden** on the south side of the house, which was the pride of Mrs. Lee. A latticed arbor that once stood at the center of the garden was used by the family for entertaining, reading, painting, and relaxing in summer.

On the far side of the garden, pick up the brick path adjacent to the road and follow it to the left. Through the hedge, enter the:

25. **Tomb of the Unknown Civil War Dead,** where some 2,111 Confederate and Union soldiers were buried in September 1866. They fell in battle at Bull Run and along the route to the Rappahannock River.

From here, walk to the road and down the hill, past the:

26. **Old Amphitheater,** a white colonnade with a latticed roof and center dais where memorial services and special ceremonies were held from 1868 to 1921, when it could no longer accommodate the many people who wanted to attend. The old amphitheater held 1,500 spectators, whereas the new one can accommodate 5,000. It is now used for

about 15 or 20 smaller ceremonies and commemorative events during the year.

From here, follow Meigs Avenue to one of the oldest and most beautiful parts of the cemetery, designated:

27. **Section 1,** where soldiers from the Revolutionary and Civil wars are buried, among them **Absolom Baird** (1824–1905), who fought in numerous Civil War battles including Manassas, Yorktown, Williamsburg, Chickamauga, Chattanooga, Atlanta, and Savannah. Also in Section 1 is the grave of **Col. Abner Doubleday** (1819–93), a Civil War hero who fought in South Carolina, Maryland, and Virginia. Doubleday has been credited with inventing the game of baseball (the Doubleday Field in Cooperstown, New York, is named for him, and the Baseball Hall of Fame and Museum there honors him). The truth is, Abner didn't invent the game, but he did found the nation's first cable-car company, in San Francisco. Further along, a tan obelisk marks the grave of **Brig. Gen. Stephen Vincent Benet** (1827–95); behind Benet's marker, a large monument indicates the final resting place of **Quartermaster Gen. Montgomery Meigs** (1816–92). Directly in front of it is the smaller tomb of Meigs' son, John (the reclining figure on top represents him), who was killed in the Civil War when he was 20 years old. General Meigs, a staunch Unionist, was furious over the decision of Robert E. Lee, a fellow southerner he had known for more than 20 years, to leave the Union army and join ranks with the Confederates. He chose Arlington, Lee's home, for the nation's cemetery, knowing that the presence of graves here would deter the Lee family from ever returning. (He was right.) An engineer and architect, Meigs also designed the Old Pension Building in Judiciary Square, the ornate Old Executive Office Building near the White House, and what is now the Centennial Building of the Smithsonian Institution.

Follow Meigs Avenue to McPherson Avenue and turn left onto it.

To the right, you'll notice that many Civil War graves are inscribed simply "Unknown U.S. Soldier"; body-identification methods were not very good in the 19th century. When the road divides, walk to your right. When you come to a road, cross it, and walk towards the stone wall in a direct line from the Section 15 marker, passing the grave of Frank Antos in the shape of a cross. Near the wall, a slanted marker, its metal frontpiece turquoise with patina, is the gravestone of:

28. **James Parks** (1843–1929), a former slave and the only person buried in the cemetery who was born and died on the property. Members of the Parks family were slaves here under Mr. Custis, who in his will decreed that all the slaves be freed within five years of his death, which occurred in 1857. When the Lee family left Arlington House in 1861, the slaves remained; Parks chose to stay after the Union troops arrived. After the Civil War, he stayed on, working as a maintenance person for the cemetery, a job he held until he died. Because of his special relationship with Arlington, and his lifetime devotion to it, Parks is the only non-military person buried here. A special marker designates his grave.

Back at the spot where the road divides, take the left fork; graves from World War I, World War II, Korea, and Vietnam will be on your right. When you come to the junction of McPherson and Garfield Drives, bear left and walk past Farragut Avenue. Coming up on your right at Jackson Circle is Section 1b, the:

29. **Confederate Section of the Cemetery and the Confederate Monument,** a statue of a female figure holding a laurel branch. About 410 Confederate soldiers who died behind Yankee lines (along with some Confederate wives, civilians, and unknowns) fill this section, which was set aside in 1900, after some of the hard feelings between North and South had died down. The monument was erected in 1914, on the anniversary of the birthday of Jefferson Davis, president of the Confederacy. It was designed by sculptor and Confederate veteran Moses Ezekiel, who is buried at its base. The Confederate graves form circles around the monument; note that the markers have pointed tops—to keep the Yankees from sitting on them, some Southerners muse.

Farther down this road, on your left, is the granite:

30. **Rough Riders Monument,** erected in 1906 to the memory of the feisty brigade (whose real name was the First U.S. Volunteer Cavalry) that fought during the Spanish-American War. The most famous Rough Rider, Theodore Roosevelt, attended the unveiling ceremony.

From here retrace your steps to Farragut Avenue and turn right. When you get to Sigsbee Avenue, turn right to visit the:

31. **Mast of the USS Maine,** placed here in 1912 as part of a memorial to the *Maine* and the 229 crewmen and officers who died when it was blown up in Havana Harbor on February 15, 1898, an incident that precipitated U.S. involvement in the Spanish-American War. The bodies of those who died in the explosion were reinterred in Arlington Cemetery in 1899; the mast, all that could be seen of the sunken ship, stood in Havana Harbor for 12 years before it was removed to Arlington. It rests on a battleship-style turret, with the names of the dead inscribed around it. Half the ship's bell is on the inner door. The anchor in front of the memorial, from the Boston Navy Yard, is similar to the original one from the *Maine.*

Appropriately, from here you can glimpse the Corinthian column of the:

32. **Spanish-American War Memorial,** topped with a globe and eagle. It was dedicated by Theodore Roosevelt on May 21, 1902. The war brought Southerners and Northerners together under a common battle cry—"Remember the *Maine*"—for the first time since the Civil War. If you want a better look at it, walk over after Stop 36.

Follow the walkway from the mast of the Maine to the street. You'll pass on your right a:

33. **marker in Honor of Ignace Jan Paderewski,** erected by the American Legion in remembrance of the "artist, composer, musician, statesman, patriot, humanitarian, and friend of American war veterans, who from his death until the rebirth of freedom in his homeland here rested in honor and dignity, now may his soul be eternally at peace and his memory entombed in the land of his fathers, a free Poland." Paderewski had requested that he be laid to rest in

Arlington until his country was free. His body lay in the vault of the USS *Maine* Memorial from 1941 until June 27, 1992, when it was removed, to be reinterred in his native Poland.

At the end of this path, to the left are two monuments. First is the:

34. **memorial to the eight servicemen** who died in an aircraft accident attempting to rescue 53 American hostages in Iran on April 25, 1980 (three of the men are buried at Arlington).

Here you'll also come across the:

35. ***Challenger* Memorial,** honoring the crew of the *Challenger,* which exploded soon after lift-off in 1986.

From here, walk to the road, turn right, and soon you'll come to a flagstone walkway under a tall tree. Beside the path is the:

36. **grave of Audie Murphy** (1924–71), marked by a simple headstone among many others. Short and plucky, Murphy, an actor, was also a major in the Texas infantry and the most decorated soldier in World War II. Among the 28 medals he won during World War II—all before his 21st birthday—was the prestigious Congressional Medal of Honor. His acting career followed his fame as a soldier, and he even got to play himself in the movie *To Hell and Back.* He met an untimely death in a plane crash at the age of 46.

From here, cross the street to visit the:

37. **Memorial Amphitheater.** Woodrow Wilson laid the cornerstone for the white marble structure with its striking Doric colonnade in 1915. It was dedicated on Memorial Day in 1920, and seats 5,000 people—up to 300 on the stage alone, above which are Abraham Lincoln's words from the Gettysburg Address: " . . . We here highly resolve that these dead shall not have died in vain." Around the amphitheater's exterior wall are the names of 44 battles fought during wars in which the United States was involved, from the Revolutionary War through the Spanish-American War. If you arrive on Memorial Day, Veterans Day, or Easter Sunday, expect to find a memorial service—and a large crowd—here. (On Memorial Day weekend, miniature

American flags fly on all 225,000 graves, an incredibly moving sight.) The construction of the amphitheater was the idea of a Civil War group, the Grand Army of the Republic, that felt the need for a permanent structure befitting the national significance of the cemetery.

Funeral services are rarely held here. A few exceptions have been Moses Ezekiel, sculptor of the Confederate Monument, in 1921; Polish statesman Ignace Jan Paderewski, in 1941; and Army Gen. John J. Pershing, in 1948.

Adjacent to the amphitheater is the:

38. **Tomb of the Unknowns,** which started out with the remains of a soldier from World War I, interred here on Armistice Day, November 11, 1921. On Memorial Day, 1954, an unknown soldier from World War II and the Korean War were also interred here, to be joined on Memorial Day, 1984, by an unknown soldier from the Vietnam War. All branches of the armed services are represented, and all those who did not return home from the wars remembered in the words inscribed on the tomb: "Here rests in honored glory an American soldier known but to God." The tomb is watched over by a 24-hour honor guard: a single soldier, who takes 21 steps in front of the tomb, pauses 21 seconds to face it, turns, pauses another 21 seconds, then repeats the process in the other direction (the number 21 refers to the military's highest honor, the 21-gun salute). The solemn changing of the guard ceremony takes place every half hour during the summer, every hour on the hour during the winter, and every two hours at night.

Awards and tributes that have been given to the unknown soldiers, and a pictorial history of their burials, are on view in a special memorial display hall in the amphitheater.

Exit this area by the flagstone path to the right of the tomb, and circle around to your left. Face the steps for a beautiful view of the tomb with the amphitheater behind it. Pass the two main walkways that lead to the tomb, and turn right at Section 7A. On the right, just before you link up with Roosevelt Drive, is the:

39. **grave of Joe Louis** (1914–81). The pink granite marker states "Louis, The Brown Bomber, World Heavyweight Champion, 1937–1949," and has a figure of Louis in a

fighting stance. To date, Louis has held this title longer than any other boxer. He served the United States in World War II, joining the same segregated unit as baseball star Jackie Robinson.

Turn left onto Roosevelt Drive and follow it back to the Visitors Center (the way is well marked with blue signs). En route, just below Grant Avenue, you'll see the:

40. **equestrian statue** (one of only two in the cemetery) of **Field Marshall Sir John Dill** (1881–1944), the senior British representative on the Combined Chiefs of Staff for the Allies from 1941 until his death. Dill, who was originally from Northern Ireland and was knighted by King George VI in 1942, was instrumental in getting the British and American forces to cooperate during World War II. The regard in which Americans held him resulted in his being buried at Arlington.

If you want to visit the:

41. **Iwo Jima Statue,** just outside of Arlington Cemetery, retrace your steps from the Kennedy graves to Custis Walk and turn right. You'll pass Robert Todd Lincoln's grave again and then walk for about 20 minutes. The large bronze statue honors all marines who have died in battle since 1775, when the Marine Corps was founded. It was modeled after an Associated Press, Pulitzer Prize–winning photograph that appeared in newspapers worldwide, showing six U.S. servicemen struggling to raise the American flag on Mount Suribachi during the battle of Iwo Jima (Japan) in World War II. Three of the marines depicted in the photo and the sculpture died during the month-long battle; three are buried at Arlington. The sculpture, which weighs 100 tons, is the largest cast bronze figure in the world.

Nearby is the:

42. **Netherlands Carillon,** a gift from the Netherlands to the United States in 1954 in gratitude for its support during and after World War II. If you arrive on a Saturday afternoon or a national holiday, you're likely to hear melodies wafting across the hills from the 49 carillon bells (you can also climb the tower to see the carillonneur at work).

From here follow Custis Walk back to the main road, turn left, and return to the Information Center or the Metro.

Take a Break The bad news is there's really not a refreshment stop at or near the cemetery. The good news is that the Metro awaits you 200 yards from the cemetery gate and will take you back to Washington, where dining options are numerous. Check other walking tours in this book for additional suggestions.

You might take the Metro to Dupont Circle (changing for the Red Line at Metro Center) and head for the **Iron Gate Restaurant & Garden,** 1734 N Street NW (tel. 202/737-1370). Housed in a converted 19th-century stable, the Iron Gate, with its blazing brick fireplace, is Washington's coziest venue on chilly days. And if the weather is fine, you can dine alfresco under a grape-and-wisteria arbor in an enchanting brick-walled garden. Entrées—which run the gamut from superb pasta dishes (such as tagliatelle with grilled shrimp, pancetta, and peas in a balsamic vinaigrette) to crisp-skinned roast free-range chicken (the best I've ever had) with herbed-rice pilaf and golden raisin/pine-nut sauce—come with fresh-baked focaccia breads infused with herbs, sun-dried tomato, walnuts, or parmesan. There's an excellent wine list, and "celestial desserts" include a first-rate tiramisù. Prices are moderate. Open for lunch Monday through Friday from 11:30am to 5pm, dinner Monday through Saturday from 5 to 10pm, Sunday brunch from 10:30am to 2:30pm and Sunday dinner from 5 to 9pm (open on Sundays only April through mid-September).

Or get off at Metro Center for the **Old Ebbitt Grill,** 675 15th St, NW, between F and G Streets (tel. 347-4801). See Walking Tour 2, "Monuments and Memorials," for details.

OLD TOWN ALEXANDRIA

Start: Ramsay House.

Directions: Alexandria, Virginia, is five miles south of Washington, D.C., and easily accessible by Metro. Take the Yellow or Blue Line to King Street station, picking up a transfer at your departure station. From King Street station, you can catch a bus to Ramsay House; ask the station attendant which one to take.

Finish: Waterfront Park.

Time: Approximately 3 to 5 hours, depending on how many tours you take and how much time you spend browsing in shops.

Best Times: Any day except Monday, when several attractions are closed. Weekends can be crowded, so weekday visits are preferable.

History thrives in Alexandria. Founded by a group of Scottish tobacco merchants in 1749, this colonial port is proud of its heritage as the hometown of George Washington and Robert E. Lee. Many of its streets still bear colonial names such as Prince, King, and Royal. In the Old Town historic district—"a mother lode of Americana"—over 2,000 18th- and 19th-century buildings have been restored or reconstructed in an ongoing program of archaeological and historic research. And capitalizing on the great volume of tourism generated by these restorations are dozens of restaurants, antique shops, art galleries, and charming boutiques. A day spent strolling Old Town's brick sidewalks and cobblestone streets is both educational and delightful. I encourage you to take all the guided tours available.

● ● ● ● ● ● ● ● ● ● ● ● ● ● ● ●

Starting Out   You might plan to arrive early in Alexandria and fortify yourself with a hearty pre-tour breakfast at the **Holiday Inn,** 480 King Street (ask the bus driver where to get off; it's a short walk from here to our first stop). This Holiday Inn has plenty of historic Old Town charm, most notably in its plant-filled, mahogany-paneled, Palladian-windowed dining room. In good weather, there's also outdoor seating on a brick courtyard. A big buffet breakfast is served from 6:30am Monday through Saturday (it's especially elaborate on Saturdays); Sundays a champagne brunch buffet is served from 10:30am to 2:30pm. Prices are very reasonable, and you can also order à la carte. For details call 703/549-6080.

Start at:

1. **Ramsay House,** 221 King Street, at Fairfax Street. The Alexandria Convention & Visitors Bureau (tel. 703/838-4200) is located in Alexandria's oldest house (1724), which is complete with Dutch gambrel roof and English garden. It was the home of the city's founder, first Lord Mayor, and esteemed friend of George Washington, William Ramsay. His wife, Anne, was commended by Thomas Jefferson for raising over $75,000 in funds to support the American Revolution. Here you can purchase a block ticket for reduced-price admission to four historic Alexandria properties (Carlyle House, Gadsby's Tavern, Lee's Boyhood Home, and the Lee-Fendall House), pick up maps and brochures (they're available in many languages), see a 13-minute video about Alexandria history, and find out about special events taking place during your visit. If you came by car, a free 24-hour parking permit is available as well. Ramsay House is open daily from 9am to 5pm.

When you leave Ramsay House, cross Fairfax Street diagonally and take it to no. 105, the:

2. **Stabler-Leadbeater Apothecary,** a landmark pharmacy that was in continuous operation from 1792 to 1933 (its building dates to 1775). Today it functions as a museum, its shelves lined with hundreds of antique medicine bottles, old scales stamped with the royal crown, mortars and pestles, patent remedies, and bloodletting equipment. Robert E. Lee, who purchased the paint for his Arlington, Virginia, home here, was on the premises when J. E. B. Stuart strode in and handed him the order from the War Department to proceed at once to Harper's Ferry and end the John Brown insurrection. And among the documentary records on display is this 1802 missive from Mount Vernon: "Mrs. Washington desires Mr. Stabler will send by the bearer a quart bottle of his best Castor Oil and the bill for it." The apothecary was a meeting place for politicians like Henry Clay, Daniel Webster, and John Calhoun, who gathered here to discuss events of the day while waiting for the ferry to return to Washington. During the War of 1812 the store was ransacked by the British navy. Note the globes of colored water in the window; they were supposed to have warned the illiterate (via differing hues) of epidemics like plague, yellow fever, and cholera. A five-minute recording elucidates exhibits. Among other things, you'll learn about 18th- and 19th-century drugs, which were mostly made of leaves, berries, roots, and bark.

Open Monday through Saturday from 10am to 4pm, Sunday from 1 to 5pm.

A small admission is charged, and the adjoining gift shop uses its proceeds to maintain the apothecary.

Now double back on Fairfax Street to no. 121, on your right between King and Cameron Streets, where you'll find:

3. **Carlyle House.** Prominent Scottish-born merchant John Carlyle (1720–80) built this impressive Palladian-style mansion—patterned after Scottish and English manor houses—between 1751 and 1753. It was a waterfront property then, with its own wharf (landfill later changed that), and a social and political center visited by many notables. Carlyle helped his friend George Washington mill his wheat and ship it to England; when he was in town, Washington visited almost every Sunday after church. The already-wealthy Carlyle married Sarah Fairfax of Belvoir,

Old Town Alexandria

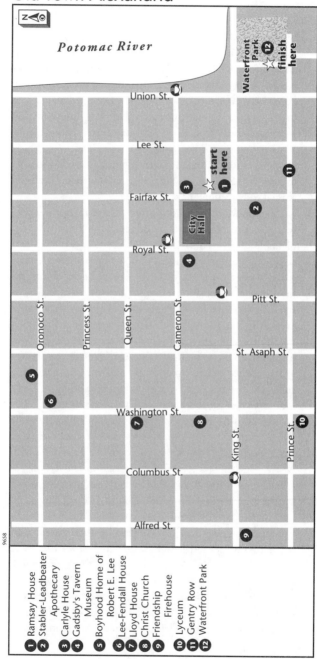

N

Potomac River

Waterfront Park

12 finish here

Union St.

Lee St.

3 start here **1**

Fairfax St.

2

City Hall

Royal St.

4

Pitt St.

Oronoco St.

Princess St.

Queen St.

Cameron St.

St. Asaph St.

11

5

6

Washington St.

7 **8**

King St.

Prince St.

10

Columbus St.

Alfred St.

9

9658

1. Ramsay House
2. Stabler-Leadbeater Apothecary
3. Carlyle House
4. Gadsby's Tavern Museum
5. Boyhood Home of Robert E. Lee
6. Lee-Fendall House
7. Lloyd House
8. Christ Church
9. Friendship Firehouse
10. Lyceum
11. Gentry Row
12. Waterfront Park

daughter of one of the most influential men in the Colony, whose dowry included thousands of acres of land. Sarah's British uncle, Thomas Lord Fairfax, owned over six million acres of land in Northern Virginia! And Carlyle himself, in addition to this house, owned three working plantations where he raised wheat and corn and bred racehorses. The exquisitely carved woodwork, swans' neck pediments over the doorways, and beautiful Palladian window on the stairway are all typical of Virginia's finest 18th-century architecture. As for the interior, it was equal in grandeur to the exterior; as a trader with Europe, Carlyle was able to import the best furnishings and appointments available abroad to his Virginia home.

An important meeting occurred here in April, 1755, when Maj. Gen. Edward Braddock, commander-in-chief of His Majesty's Forces in North America, met with five colonial governors and asked them to help finance a campaign against the French and Indians. The governors' refusal of this proposition was one of the first instances of serious friction between America and Britain that would eventually lead to the Revolution. Nevertheless, Braddock made Carlyle House his headquarters during the campaign, during which time he badly abused the house and its servants. Carlyle was less than impressed with his guest. He called the general "a man of weak understanding . . . very indolent . . . slave to his passions, women and wine."

The house is meant to show how a gentleman of means lived at the end of the 18th century. Tours (given every half hour, with the latest at 4:30pm) begin in the servant's hall, where you'll hear a recorded conversation between slaves Charles and Penny (mannequins) and pick up a 22-pound bucket of water like those slaves routinely carried upstairs. Also on view are the family dining room, several bedrooms, the central passageway (used for large gatherings, with an orchestra on the stair landing), the large parlor (the most formal room in the house), the family sitting room, and a room that is set up to show the architectural structure of the house. Open Tuesday through Saturday from 10am to 4:30pm, Sunday noon to 4:30pm. Admission is charged.

Upon exiting, make a left on Cameron Street and walk a block to:

4. **Gadsby's Tavern Museum,** 134 North Royal Street. Consisting of two buildings—a 1770 Georgian tavern and the adjoining Federal-style 1792 City Tavern and Hotel—Gadsby's was the social center of 18th-century Alexandria. The buildings are named for English tavern-keeper John Gadsby, who operated them very successfully from 1796 to 1808. Here itinerant merchants hawked their wares, doctors and dentists administered to a hapless clientele (these were rudimentary professions in the 18th century), and all manner of entertainment took place. George and Martha Washington danced in the second-floor ballroom—the setting for many lavish parties—and the tavern was visited by James Madison, Lafayette, John Adams, John Quincy Adams, and Thomas Jefferson. Washington had a kitchenless townhouse nearby, so he often ate here as well. Today—thanks to modern excavations and detailed colonial inventories—the rooms are restored to their 18th-century appearance. You'll get a feel for the very unluxurious life of guests at an 18th-century inn, who purchased not a bed, but a space on a bed (or the floor) shared by several strangers. Hence, since many travelers stayed at hostelries such as this one during political meetings, the expression "politics makes strange bedfellows" arose.

Thirty-minute tours depart 15 minutes before and after the hour, with the final tour at 4:15pm or 3:15pm, depending on the time of year. April through September tours depart between 10:15am and 4:15pm Tuesday through Saturday, 1:15 to 4:15pm on Sunday; October through March 11:15am to 3:15pm, with Sunday tours between 1:15 and 3:15pm. Admission is charged.

Take a Break When you enter **Gadsby's Tavern Restaurant,** 138 North Royal Street, at Cameron Street (tel. 703/548-1288), you'll pass through the portals where Washington reviewed his troops and dine off pewter plates on colonial fare. Lunch here might begin with soup from the stockpot served with homemade sourdough crackers, continue with a sandwich of sliced turkey breast with Virginia ham and bacon on Sally Lunn bread, and conclude with a dessert of buttermilk "pye." Unfinished yellow-pine plank floors, 18th-century furnishings, tables lit by hurricane lamps, and servers in colonial costume enhance the period ambience. Prices are moderate at lunch, a bit more at dinner. Open for lunch Monday through Saturday from 11:30am to 3pm, Sunday brunch from 11am to 3pm, and dinner nightly (with strolling minstrels and balladeers) from 5:30 to 10pm. Reservations are recommended at dinner.

From Gadsby's Tavern Museum, walk back to Cameron Street and turn left, noting no. 508 (a replica of George Washington's Alexandria townhouse on its original site). Make a right on St. Asaph Street and a left on Oronoco Street en route to the:

5. **Boyhood Home of Robert E. Lee,** 607 Oronoco Street, built between 1793 and 1795. Revolutionary cavalry hero Henry "Light Horse Harry" Lee brought his wife, Ann Hill Carter, and their five children to live in this early Federal-style mansion in 1812. At that time the future Confederate military leader was just a boy of five. Earlier residents Col. and Mrs. William Fitzhugh were friends of George Washington, an occasional guest. Since 1824, when Lafayette visited Ann Hill Carter Lee (by then the widow of his comrade-in-arms) at the house, the elegant drawing room has been known as the Lafayette Room. The Lee home was made into a museum in 1967. Be sure to see the garden with its 200-year-old magnolia tree and wisteria arbor.

Tours are given Monday through Saturday from 10am to 3:30pm, on Sunday from 1 to 3:30pm. Admission is charged.

Diagonally across the street is the:

6. **Lee-Fendall House,** 614 Oronoco Street. This handsome white clapboard residence—its original Federal architecture extensively renovated in 1850 in the Greek Revival style—was home to 37 members of the Lee family between 1785 and 1903. The house was built by Phillip Richard Fendall, one of the founders of the Bank of Alexandria. During his lifetime he married three Lee women (consecutively, of course). Both George Washington and "Light Horse Harry" Lee were frequent visitors to the house. It was here that Lee wrote Alexandria's farewell address to Washington and, later,

penned Washington's famous funeral oration ("First in war, first in peace, and first in the hearts of his countrymen"). During the Civil War the house was seized for use as a Union hospital. It is entered through a pretty colonial garden with magnolia and chestnut trees, roses, and boxwood-lined paths. Much of the interior woodwork and glass is original. The house is furnished to reflect life in the Victorian era.

Open Tuesday through Saturday from 10am to 3:45pm, Sunday from noon to 3:45pm, with 30-minute tours departing throughout the day.

From Oronoco, turn left onto Washington Street. At the right-hand corner across Queen Street is:

7. **Lloyd House,** 220 North Washington Street, a beautiful late-Georgian residence (1797) that was originally used as a school by Quaker schoolmaster Benjamin Hallowell. Robert E. Lee was a student here. The house was sold in 1832 to John Lloyd, whose wife, Anne, was a first cousin of Robert E. Lee. Today it is part of the Alexandria Library and houses a fascinating collection of old documents, books, and records on the city and state. The house is open Monday through Friday from 9am to 6pm, Saturday from 9am to 5pm. A docent will show you around.

Proceed farther south on Washington Street, and cross Cameron Street to the tranquil graveyard entrance behind:

8. **Christ Church,** where both George Washington and Robert E. Lee worshipped (you can sit in their family pews). This sturdy red-brick church has been in continuous use since 1773, and its original structure and hand-blown windows remain intact. During the 18th century Washington and others discussed revolution in the churchyard, and, at the start of the Civil War, Robert E. Lee met here with Richmond representatives who offered him command of Virginia's military forces. American presidents generally attend a service here on a Sunday close to Washington's birthday and sit in his pew. Franklin Delano Roosevelt and Winston Churchill attended services at Christ Church on the World Day of Prayer shortly after Pearl Harbor was bombed.

The church is open Monday through Friday from 9am to 4pm, Saturday from 9am to 3pm, Sunday from 2 to

"... First in the Hearts of His Countrymen"

Though Alexandria calls itself George Washington's hometown, it was never his primary residence. He did spend a great deal of time here, though. As a 17-year-old surveyor, he helped lay out the town. As an adult, he had a home on Cameron Street, worshipped at Christ Church, trained his troops in Market Square, and bid them farewell at Gadsby's Tavern.

Born into a Virginia planter family in 1732, George Washington pursued his lifelong interest in military arts from an early age. At 22, he was already a lieutenant colonel fighting for the British in the French and Indian War. An aide to General Braddock (see Stop 3), he escaped injury, though four bullets rent his coat and two horses were shot from under him. Like many Virginia planters, however, he began to feel exploited by the British government. On July 3, 1775, he assumed command of the Continental Army, a position he would hold for six years.

After the British surrender at Yorktown, Washington—respected as a great military hero—retired to his Potomac estate, Mount Vernon. However, he was unable to ignore the needs of the fledgling nation for which he had fought so valiantly. He agreed to preside over the 1787 Constitutional Convention. Washington also reluctantly accepted the presidency, taking office on April 30, 1789. His presidency was unique in that every action set traditions for the new republic. "As the first of everything . . . will serve to establish a Precedent," he wrote James Madison, "it is devoutly wished on my part that these precedents may be fixed on true principles."

Washington finally retired to Mount Vernon in 1797, two years before his death. He is buried there next to his wife Martha. Of all tributes to Washington, I like best that of Abigail Adams: "He never grew giddy, but ever maintained a modest diffidence of his own talents. . . . Possessed of power, possessed of an extensive influence, he never used it but for the benefit of his country. . . . If we look through the whole tenor of his life, history will not produce to us a parallel."

4:30pm. There's usually a docent on hand to give brief lectures to visitors, but there's no formal tour.

Take a Break **South Austin Grill,** 801 King Street, at South Columbus Street (tel. 703/684-8969), features totally authentic Tex-Mex fare—lime-marinated mesquite-grilled fajitas, crabmeat quesadillas, tacos al carbòn, and more. It's all superb, and prices are moderate. Arrive off hours to avoid a long wait for seating at this deservedly popular restaurant. They don't take reservations. Open Sunday through Thursday from 11:30am to 11pm, Friday and Saturday from 11:30am to midnight.

From the front entrance of Christ Church turn left on Columbus Street, and make a right on King Street on your way to:

9. **Friendship Firehouse,** 107 South Alfred Street. This historic firehouse, dating from 1774, has a collection of antique firefighting equipment on view. First-floor engine room exhibits include 19th-century speaking trumpets used to bark out commands, leather hoses, antique buckets and axes, ornate hand-drawn fire carts, and a 1770 fire engine. Upstairs, furnished in Victorian style, is the company meeting room (in addition to its practical function, the Friendship Fire Company was a fraternal organization). Open Friday and Saturday from 10am to 4pm, Sunday from 1 to 4pm.

Walk south on Alfred Street to Prince Street and make a left. At the corner of Prince and Washington Streets is the Greek Revival:

10. **Lyceum,** built in 1839 as the city's first cultural center. During the Civil War, Union forces used the building as a hospital. Today it is a museum focusing on Alexandria's history from colonial times through the 20th century. An adjoining shop carries needlepoint patterns, 18th-century reproductions, and other quaint wares. The Lyceum additionally serves as an information office about Virginia state attractions. It's open Monday through Saturday from 10am to 5pm, Sunday from 1 to 5pm.

A few blocks farther east on Prince Street, between Fairfax and Lee Streets, is:

11. **Gentry Row,** named for the leading citizens who made their homes in these three-story townhouses in the 18th and 19th centuries.

    Continue east along Prince Street to:

12. **Waterfront Park,** overlooking the Potomac. When it's in port (usually spring through fall) the Scandinavian schooner *Alexandria* is docked here and offers free weekend tours above and below deck. Other times, simply enjoy a pleasant stroll along the waterfront.

    Winding Down   **Radio Free Italy,** 5 Cameron Street (tel. 703/683-0361), is part of a waterfront dining complex. It consists of a downstairs carryout operation and a fancier upstairs dining room with windows overlooking the boat-filled harbor. Both levels also feature alfresco seating. Prices are moderate. The fare includes oak-fired California-style pizzas, fabulous homemade pastas, and decadent desserts. Open Sunday through Thursday from 11:30am to 10pm, Friday and Saturday from 11:30am to 11pm.

    When you're heading back to the King Street station, another great choice is the **Hard Times Café,** 1404 King Street, near South West Street (tel. 703/683-5340). It's the local headquarters for cookoff-winning chili served with oven-fresh cornbread—as good as any you'll get in Texas. A great choice for families. Prices are low and the ambience—country music, roomy booth seating, Lone Star flags, and historic photos of the Old West on the walls—is attractive. Open Monday through Friday from 11:30am to 11pm, Saturday from noon to 11pm, and Sunday from noon to 10pm.

ESSENTIALS &
RECOMMENDED READING

Washington is one of America's most delightful cities—a fitting site for the nation's capital. It's a city designed for strolling, offering both natural beauty and stunning architecture. Learning your way around is quick and easy.

ORIENTATION/CITY LAYOUT

Pierre Charles L'Enfant designed Washington's great sweeping avenues crossed by numbered and lettered streets. At key intersections he placed spacious circles. Although the circles are enhanced with monuments, statuary, and fountains, L'Enfant planned them with a dual motive—they were also designed to serve as strategic command posts to ward off invaders or marauding mobs. After what had happened in Paris during the French Revolution—and remember, that was current history at the time—his design views were most practical.

Neighborhoods in Brief

The Mall   This lovely tree-lined stretch of open space between Constitution and Independence Avenues, extending for 2¹/₂ miles from the Capitol to the Lincoln Memorial, is the hub of tourist attractions. It includes most of the Smithsonian Institution museums, and many other visitor attractions are close by. The 300-foot-wide Mall is used by natives as well as tourists—joggers, food vendors, kite-flyers, and picnickers among them. It's also the setting for festivals and occasional baseball games.

Downtown Roughly the area between 7th and 22nd Streets NW going east to west, and P Street and Pennsylvania Avenue going north to south, downtown is a mix of Federal Triangle's government office buildings, K Street and Connecticut Avenue restaurants and shopping, F Street department stores, and much more. Too large an area to have a consistent character, it contains lovely Lafayette Park, Washington's tiny porno district, its slightly larger Chinatown, the Convention Center, and a half dozen or so sightseeing attractions.

Capitol Hill Everyone's heard of "the Hill," the area crowned by the Capitol. When people speak of Capitol Hill they refer to a large section of town, extending from the western side of the Capitol to RFK Memorial Stadium going east, bounded by H Street NE and the Southwest Freeway north and south. It contains not only the chief symbol of the nation's capital, but the Supreme Court building, the Library of Congress, the Folger Shakespeare Library, Union Station, and the Botanic Gardens. Much of it is a quiet residential neighborhood of tree-lined streets and Victorian homes. Many restaurants are in the vicinity.

Foggy Bottom The area west of the White House to the edge of Georgetown, Foggy Bottom was Washington's early industrial center. Its name comes from the foul fumes emitted in those days by a coal depot and gasworks, but its original name, Funkstown (for owner Jacob Funk), is perhaps even worse. There's nothing foul about the area today. The Kennedy Center and George Washington University are located here. Constitution and Pennsylvania Avenues are Foggy Bottom's southern and northern boundaries, respectively.

Dupont Circle Generally, when Washingtonians speak of Dupont Circle they don't mean just the park, they mean the area around it. The park itself, named for Rear Adm. Samuel Francis du Pont of the U.S. Navy, is centered around D.C.'s most famous fountain, at the intersection of Connecticut and Massachusetts Avenues, and is a popular rendezvous spot. Dupont Circle is one of the liveliest sections in town, rivaled only by Georgetown for nightspots, movie theaters, and restaurants.

Georgetown   This historic community dates back to Colonial times. It was a thriving tobacco port long before the District of Columbia was formed, and one of its attractions, the Old Stone House, dates to pre-Revolutionary days. Georgetown action centers on M and Wisconsin Streets NW, where you'll find numerous boutiques, chic restaurants, and popular pubs. But do get off the main drags and see the quiet tree-lined streets of restored colonial row houses, stroll through the beautiful gardens of Dumbarton Oaks, and check out the C&O Canal. One of the reasons so much activity flourishes in Georgetown is that it contains the campus of Georgetown University.

Adams-Morgan   This unconventional multiethnic neighborhood (it's easy to be unconventional in D.C.; all you have to do is not wear a suit and tie) is popular for its restaurants serving Jamaican, Ethiopian, Spanish, and other international cuisines. Try to plan at least one meal up here; it's a good opportunity to see an authentic untouristy Washington neighborhood. Adams-Morgan centers around Columbia Road and 18th Street NW.

Main Arteries & Streets

The primary artery of Washington is **Pennsylvania Avenue,** scene of parades, inaugurations, and other splashy events. Pennsylvania runs northwest in a direct line between the Capitol and the White House. In the original plan, the president was supposed to have an uninterrupted view of the Capitol from the White House. But Andrew Jackson placed the Treasury Building between the White House and the Capitol, blocking the presidential vista. Pennsylvania Avenue continues on a northwest angle to Georgetown from the White House.

Constitution Avenue, paralleled to the south most of the way by **Independence Avenue,** runs east-west flanking the Capitol and the Mall with its many major museums and important government buildings to the north and south.

Washington's longest avenue, **Massachusetts Avenue,** runs north of and parallel to Pennsylvania. Along the way you'll find Union Station and Dupont Circle, central to the area known as Embassy Row. Farther out are the Naval Observatory (the vice president's residence is on the premises), Washington

National Cathedral, and American University. Massachusetts Avenue just keeps going, right into Maryland.

Connecticut Avenue, running more directly north, starts at Lafayette Square directly facing the White House. It's the city's Fifth Avenue, the boulevard with elegant eateries, posh boutiques, and expensive hotels.

Wisconsin Avenue, from the point where it crosses M Street, is downtown Georgetown. Antique shops, trendy boutiques, discos, restaurants, and pubs all vie for attention. Yet somehow Georgetown manages to keep its almost European charm.

GETTING AROUND

Washington is one of the easiest towns in the country to navigate. Only New York rivals its comprehensive transportation system, but Washington's clean, efficient subways put the Big Apple's underground nightmare to shame. There's also a complex bus system with routes covering all major D.C. arteries, and it's easy to hail a taxi anywhere at any time. Finally, Washington—especially the areas of interest to tourists—is pretty compact, and often the best way to get from here to there is on foot.

By Metro

The Metrorail stations are immaculate, cool, and attractive, with terra-cotta floors and high, vaulted ceilings; the sleek subway cars are air-conditioned, carpeted, furnished with upholstered seats, and fitted with picture windows; the tracks are rubber-cushioned so the ride is quiet; the service is frequent enough so you usually get a seat; and the system is so simply designed that a 10-year-old can understand it.

Metrorail's 74 stations and 89 miles of track (83 stations and 103 miles of track are the eventual goal) include locations at or near almost every sightseeing attraction and extend to suburban Maryland and northern Virginia. If you're in Washington even for a few days you'll probably have occasion to use the system, but if not, I suggest you create one—perhaps dinner at a Dupont Circle restaurant. The Metro is a sightseeing attraction in its own right.

There are five lines in operation at this writing, the **Red, Blue, Orange, Yellow,** and **Green Lines,** with extensions in the

The Metrorail System

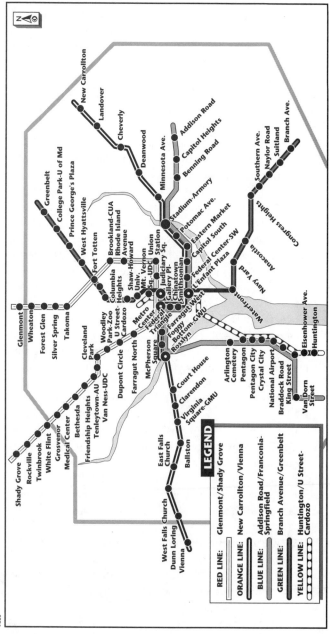

LEGEND

RED LINE: Glenmont/Shady Grove

ORANGE LINE: New Carrollton/Vienna

BLUE LINE: Addison Road/Franconia-Springfield

GREEN LINE: Branch Avenue/Greenbelt

YELLOW LINE: Huntington/U Street-Cardozo

9660

works for the future. The lines connect at several points, making transfers easy. All but Yellow and Green Line trains stop at Metro Center at 12th and F Streets; all but Red Line trains stop at L'Enfant Plaza at Maryland Avenue and 7th Street.

Metro stations are indicated by discreet brown columns bearing the station's name and topped by the letter "M." Below the "M" is a colored stripe or stripes indicating the line or lines it serves. When entering a Metro station for the first time, go to the kiosk and ask the station manager for a free copy of *All About Metro.* It contains a map of the system, explains how it works, lists parking lots at Metrorail stations, and indicates the closest Metro stops to points of interest. The station manager can also answer questions about routing or purchase of farecards.

To enter or exit a Metro station you need a computerized **farecard,** available at vending machines near the entrance. The minimum fare to enter the system is $1, which pays for rides to and from any point within seven miles of boarding during non-rush hours; during rush hours (weekdays 5:30 to 9:30am and 3 to 7pm) $1 only takes you for three miles. The maximum value allowed per card is $100. The machines take nickels, dimes, quarters, $1 bills, and $5 bills (some new machines also accept $10 and $20 bills), and they can return change. If you plan to take several Metrorail trips during your stay, put more value on the farecard to avoid having to purchase a new card each time you ride. Otherwise you might waste time standing in long lines. There's a 5% fare discount on everything you purchase over $10. Up to two children under five ride free with a paying passenger.

When you insert your card in the entrance gate, the time and location are recorded on its magnetic tape and your card is returned. Don't forget to snatch it up, and keep it handy—you have to reinsert it in the exit gate at your destination, where the fare will automatically be deducted. The card will be returned if there's any value left on it. If you arrive at a destination and your farecard doesn't have enough value, add what's necessary at the Addfare machines near the exit gate.

If you're planning to continue your travel via Metrobus, pick up a **transfer** at the station where you enter the system (*not* your destination station) from the transfer machine on the mezzanine. It's good for full fare within D.C., and gives you a discount on bus fares in Maryland and Virginia. There are no bus-to-subway transfers.

Metrorail operates Monday through Friday from 5:30am to midnight, on Saturday from 8am to midnight, and on Sunday from 10am to midnight. A Saturday or Sunday schedule is in effect on most holidays. Call 202/637-7000 for information on Metro routes.

By Bus

While any 10-year-old could understand the Metrorail system, the Metrobus system would probably perplex Einstein. The 15,800 stops on the 1,489-square-mile route (it operates on all major D.C. arteries and in the Virginia and Maryland suburbs) are indicated by red, white, and blue signs. However, the signs just tell you what buses pull into a given stop (if that), not where they go. For routing information, call 202/637-7000; a transit information agent can tell you the most efficient route from where you are to where you want to go (using bus and/or subway) almost instantly. Calls are taken daily between 6am and 11:30pm, but the line is often busy, so don't wait until the last minute to call.

If you travel the same route frequently and would like a free map and time schedule, ask the bus driver or call 202/637-7000. Information about free parking in Metrobus fringe lots is also available from this number.

As of this writing, base fare in the District is $1, and transfers are free. There are additional charges for travel into Maryland and Virginia suburbs. Bus drivers are not equipped to make change, so be sure to *carry exact change or tokens.* The latter are available at 398 ticket outlets (call 202/637-7000 for locations and hours of operation). If you will be in Washington for a while, and plan to use the buses a lot, consider a two-week pass such as the **D.C. Only Pass.** These are also available at ticket outlets. Others include zones in Virginia or Maryland.

Most buses operate daily just about around the clock. Service is very frequent on weekdays, especially during rush hours. On weekends, and late at night, your wait will be longer.

There's a full bus information center (the Metro Sales Facility) at Metro Center Station (12th and F Streets), where tokens, special bus tickets, and all else is available.

Up to two children under five ride free with a paying passenger on the Metrobus, and there are reduced fares for senior citizens (tel. 202/962-1179) and the handicapped (tel. 202/962-1245).

Should you leave something on a bus, on a train, or in a station, call Lost and Found at 202/962-1195.

By Car

Within the District a car is a luxury, as public transportation is so comprehensive. Having a car can even be an inconvenience, especially during spring and summer, when traffic jams are frequent, parking spaces almost nonexistent, and parking lots ruinously expensive. But there's a great deal to see in the D.C. vicinity, and for most attractions in Virginia and Maryland you will want a car.

All the major car-rental companies are represented here. Some handy phone numbers: **Budget** (tel. toll free 800/527-0700); **Hertz** (tel. toll free 800/654-3131); **Thrifty** (tel. toll free 800/367-2277); **Avis** (tel. toll free 800/331-1212); and **Alamo** (tel. toll free 800/327-9633).

By Taxi

Surprise! You can take taxis in Washington without busting your budget—at least in some cases. District cabs work on a zone system. If you take a trip from one point to another in the same zone, you pay just $3.20 ($2.80 within a subzone of Zone 1), regardless of the distance traveled. So it would cost you $3.20 to travel a few blocks from the U.S. Botanic Garden to the Museum of American History, the same $3.20 from the Botanic Garden all the way to Dupont Circle. They're both in Zone 1. Also in Zone 1 are most other tourist attractions: the Capitol, the White House, most of the Smithsonian, the Washington Monument, the FBI, the National Archives, the Supreme Court, the Library of Congress, the Bureau of Engraving and Printing, the Old Post Office, and Ford's Theatre. If your trip takes you into a second zone, the price is $4.40, $5.50 for a third zone, $6.60 for a fourth, and so on. You're unlikely to travel more than three zones unless you're staying in some remote section of town.

So far fares are pretty low. Here's how they can add up. There's a $1.25 charge for each additional passenger after the first, so a $3.20 Zone 1 fare becomes $6.95 for a family of four (though

Taxicab Zones

LEGEND:

Zone Fares	Single Passenger and Shared Riding Rate Per Passenger
Subzone	$2.80
1 Zone	3.20
2 Zones	4.40
3 Zones	5.50
4 Zones	6.60
5 Zones	7.60
6 Zones	8.70
7 Zones	9.80
8 Zones	10.80

Group Rates:
$1.25 extra for each additional passenger after first passenger in group

P.M.:
Rush-hour (4:00-6:30 P.M.)
Surcharge—$1.00 per trip

Radio Dispatch:
Surcharge—$1.50

NOTE: Fares are doubled during periods of snow emergency as Declared by the District of Columbia Taxicab Commission.

——— MAJOR ZONE BOUNDARIES

----- SUBZONE BOUNDARIES

one child under six can ride free). There's also a rush-hour surcharge of $1 per trip between 4 and 6:30pm weekdays. And there are surcharges as well for large pieces of luggage and for arranging a pickup by telephone.

The zone system is not used when your destination is an out-of-district address (like an airport); the fare is then based on mileage covered. You can call 331-1671 to find out the rate between any point in D.C. and an address in Virginia or Maryland. Call 767-8370 for inquiries about fares within the District.

It's generally easy to hail a taxi. There are about 8,000 cabs, and drivers are allowed to pick up as many passengers as they can comfortably fit. Expect to share. You can also call a taxi, though there is a surcharge. Try **Diamond Cab Company** (tel. 387-6200), **Yellow Cab** (tel. 544-1212), or **Capitol Cab** (tel. 546-2400).

By Tourmobile

You can save on shoe leather and see most Washington landmarks in comfort aboard Tourmobiles—open-air blue-and-white sightseeing trams that run on routes along the Mall and as far out as **Arlington National Cemetery** and even (with coach service) **Mount Vernon.**

You may take the Washington and Arlington Cemetery tour or tour Arlington Cemetery only. The former visits 15 different sights on or near the Mall and three sights at Arlington Cemetery: the gravesites of the Kennedy brothers, the Tomb of the Unknowns, and Arlington House.

Here's how the Tourmobile system works. You may board vehicles at 15 different locations:

> The White House
>
> Washington Monument/U.S. Holocaust Memorial Museum
>
> Arts & Industries Building/Hirshhorn Museum
>
> National Air and Space Museum
>
> Union Station
>
> The Capitol
>
> National Gallery of Art
>
> Museum of Natural History

Museum of American History

Bureau of Engraving and Printing

Jefferson Memorial

West Potomac Park

Kennedy Center

Lincoln Memorial/Vietnam Veterans Memorial

Arlington National Cemetery

You pay the driver when you first board the bus. Along the route, you may get off at any stop to visit monuments or buildings. When you finish exploring each area, you step aboard the next Tourmobile that comes along without extra charge. The buses travel in a loop, serving each stop every 20 to 30 minutes. One fare allows you to use the buses for a full day. Well-trained narrators give commentaries about sights along the route and answer questions. Call 202/554-7950 for details on fares and schedules.

By Old Town Trolley

A service similar to Tourmobile's is Old Town Trolleys, in operation since 1986. For a fixed price, you can get on and off these green-and-orange vehicles as many times as you like within one loop, at 16 locations in the District and Arlington National Cemetery. Most stops are at or near major sightseeing attractions, including Georgetown. Trolleys operate seven days a week, 9am to 5pm Memorial Day through Labor Day, 9am to 4pm the rest of the year. The full tour, which is narrated, takes two hours, and trolleys come by every 15 to 30 minutes. The following stops are made:

Union Station

Hyatt Regency Hotel (near the National Gallery)

Pavilion at the Old Post Office

Grand Hyatt (near Ford's Theatre)

J. W. Marriott (near the Renwick and Corcoran)

Hotel Washington (near the White House)

Capital Hilton (near the National Geographic Society)

Washington Hilton (near the Phillips Collection)

Park Gourmet Washington (near the National Zoo)

Washington National Cathedral

Georgetown Park Mall

Arlington National Cemetery

Lincoln Memorial/Vietnam Veterans Memorial

Washington Monument/U.S. Holocaust Memorial Museum

Holiday Inn Capitol Hill (near Mall museums)

Library of Congress

Tickets can be purchased at all stops except the Lincoln Memorial. Call 301/985-3020 for details on fares and schedules.

FAST FACTS Washington, D.C.

American Express   There's an American Express Travel Service office at 1150 Connecticut Avenue NW (tel. 202/457-1300).

Area Code   Within the District of Columbia, it's 202. In suburban Virginia, it's 703. In suburban Maryland, it's 410 or 301.

Bookstores   A few of my favorite Washington bookstores include: Kramerbooks & Afterwords, 1517 Connecticut Avenue NW (tel. 202/387-1462); Borders Books & Music, 18th and L Streets NW (tel. 202/466-4999); Super Crown, 11 Dupont Circle (tel. 202/319-1374); and the Yes! Bookshop, 1035 31st Street NW (tel. 202/338-7874).

Climate   Washington weather is a bit unpredictable. Winter can be pretty cold, with lots of snow. Occasionally, the weather is unexpectedly warm. Advantages of winter visits are low hotel prices and no lines at attractions.

Springtime, especially in April when the cherry trees are in bloom, is the most popular season for visitors.

In summer, heat and humidity can be high, and if you aren't accustomed to them, you'll feel limp. Most places are air-conditioned, however.

Autumn in Washington is an unqualified delight. The weather is comfortable, the tourist throngs have abated, and I recommend it as the best time for a visit.

Congresspersons   To locate a senator or congressional representative, call the Capitol switchboard (tel. 202/224-3121).

Doctors and Dentists   An organization called Prologue (tel. toll free 800/DOCTORS) can refer you to any type of doctor or dentist you need. Phones are answered 24 hours a day. You can also call the Dental Referral Service at 202/547-7615 weekdays between 8am and 4pm.

Drugstores   CVS, Washington's major drugstore chain (with about 40 stores), has two 24-hour locations: 14th Street and Thomas Circle NW, at Vermont Avenue (tel. 202/628-0720) and Dupont Circle (tel. 202/785-1466), both with round-the-clock pharmacies. Check your phone book for other convenient locations.

Embassies and Consulates   The Australian embassy is at 1601 Massachusetts Avenue NW (tel. 202/797-3000); the Canadian embassy is located at 501 Pennsylvania Avenue NW (tel. 202/682-1740); the French embassy is at 4101 Reservoir Road NW (tel. 202/944-6000); the German embassy is at 4645 Reservoir Road NW (tel. 202/298-4000); and the embassy of the United Kingdom is at 3100 Massachusetts Avenue NW (tel. 202/462-1340).

Emergencies   Dial 911 to contact the police or fire department or to call an ambulance.

Hospitals   The emergency wards at Georgetown University Hospital, 3800 Reservoir Road NW (tel. 202/784-2118), and George Washington University Hospital, 901 23rd Street NW (entrance on Washington Circle; tel. 202/994-3884), are both excellent.

Hotel Tax   In the District, in addition to your hotel rate, you pay 11% sales tax and $1.50 per room per night in occupancy tax. At Virginia hotels sales tax is 4.5%; hotel occupancy tax varies throughout the state. In Maryland, sales tax is 5%; hotel occupancy tax varies.

Libraries   The Martin Luther King, Jr., Memorial Library, 901 G Street NW (tel. 202/727-1186) is an extensive facility. Hours vary seasonally, so call ahead.

Liquor Laws   Minimum drinking age is 21. Establishments can serve alcoholic beverages from 8am to 2am Monday through Thursday, until 2:30am Friday and Saturday, and 10am to 2am Sunday. Liquor stores are closed on Sunday.

Lost Property   Should you leave something on a bus, in a train, or in a transit station, call Lost and Found at 202/962-1195.

Maps   The Washington Visitor Information Center in the Willard Collection of Shops, Pennsylvania Avenue NW, between 14th and 15th Streets (tel. 202/789-7038), stocks a supply of free maps. For Metro maps, go to the kiosk in any station and ask the manager for a free copy of *All About Metro*, which contains a map of the system and indicates the closest Metro stops to points of interest.

Newspapers and Magazines   The major newspaper is, of course, the renowned *Washington Post*. The city's other daily is the *Washington Times*. Also informative are *Washingtonian* magazine and *The City Paper*, the latter a free newspaper available at restaurants, in bookstores, and other places around town.

Post Office   D.C.'s main post office (tel. 202/523-2628) is located opposite Union Station at Massachusetts Avenue NE and North Capitol Street.

Restrooms   Visitors can usually find public toilets in bars, restaurants, hotels, museums, department stores, and service stations.

Safety   Whenever you're traveling in an unfamiliar city, stay alert. Be aware of your immediate surroundings. Wear a moneybelt—or better yet, check valuables in a safety deposit box at your hotel. Keep a close eye on your possessions and be sure to keep them in sight when you're seated in a restaurant, theater, or other public place. Don't leave valuables in your car—even in the trunk. Every city has its criminals, and Washington is no exception. It's your responsibility to be aware and alert even in the most heavily touristed areas.

Sales Tax   In the District, in addition to your hotel rate, you pay 11% sales tax and $1.50 per room per night in occupancy tax. In Virginia, sales tax is 4.5%, while occupancy tax varies throughout the state. In suburban Maryland, sales tax is 5%, occupancy tax, 9.5%.

Tourist Information   The Convention and Visitors Association's Visitor Information Center, Pennsylvania Avenue between 14th and 15th Streets NW (tel. 202/789-7038), knows all, tells all. It's open Monday through Saturday from 9am to 5pm. Dial 202/737-8866 for a recording of events of interest to tourists.

Also be sure to visit the superb Smithsonian Information Center, 1000 Jefferson Drive SW (tel. 202/357-2700). It's a must, especially for first-time visitors to the Smithsonian.